Noble Valor

Noble Valor

What Happens When Chivalry and Heroism No Longer Exist?

Anthony Knight

Dedication

I wish to dedicate this book to my mentor, the late great Adam Roarke, who always knew the struggles I was going through when I was pursuing my acting career as a leading man years ago. Thank you for believing in me and listening to me when I really needed to talk! I'll never forget you, Adam. Next, I dedicate this book to my brother Mel, who pushed me when I was younger and ready to quit because of weak willpower and a lack of belief in myself! You took all of that and used it against me, which made me mad enough to do it. Thank you, brother, I really needed that. I also want to dedicate this book to the former CEO and one of the founders of Home Depot; it was actually after I finished reading your book Kick Up Some Dust that I realized I needed to write this book. Thank you, Bernie Marcus; your book inspired me. Next, I would like to dedicate my book to the memory of a man who was like the father I never had, Jack

Williams. You wanted me to run your company; I wish now that I would have. And my final dedication goes out to TJ Myers, a beautiful, real woman I've known for years. Thank you, TJ, for all of your belief and support you've always shown me.

Contents

Foreword

Rise Up And Hold Your Head High

It's no big secret that a man should always throw his shoulders back and hold his head high. There's an old saying: "fake it till you make it." Why do you suppose that is? Could it be true? If it isn't, then why do we continue to do it? There's a simple explanation; it's as plain as the nose on your face. What exactly do I mean by this? Think of it like this: what would have happened to the human race if all the men throughout history showed their fears and simply ran away from all dangerous situations? Would we be alive today? More than likely, probably not. Thank God society had real men who chose to make a stand even though they were more than likely scared shitless, yet never showed it!

Why? Because they faked it until they made it. They made a conscious decision to be and act like men. Everything they ever needed to successfully do this was there all along; it's written in their DNA. Now that you know it, isn't it time to do something about it? I think it is, and after you read Noble Valor, you're going to sense a connection. I believe you will be able to relate to some or all of my experiences. With only one thing in mind, it's time to be men. Believe me when I tell you that no woman is going to want you if you're physically, mentally, and emotionally weak. A real woman is looking for a real man, just like a real man only wants a real woman. I grew up in and around some very rare and extenuating circumstances. Did I let those circumstances kick me down? Nope, I rose to the occasion and always held my head high. Because that's what a man is expected to do. Look, it ain't easy being a man, especially in this day and age. But I have some good news for all of you who truly desire to awaken the warrior, the protector, the loving husband and father in you. So let's dive right in on your journey to become real men. And for the women out there who may be curious about this, be my guest and I hope you enjoy reading it.

Introduction

If what they say is true, that behind every successful man there's a great woman, then why is it that so many men and women today have become so emotionally disconnected? In a society that's become hell-bent on destroying itself due to its incoherent, non-emotional state of being, isn't it about time to go back and examine all the facts of the past, present, and future? Believe it or not, sometimes it's necessary to take a good, long look into the past to find the answers that we seek. That's actually the step I took when I decided to write Noble Valor. I took a big leap of faith to break the spell of phrases like "it is what it is" or "that's just the way it is!" The last and final one that I really can't stand the most is "we don't have a choice." We always have a choice. It's with the utmost compassion and wisdom that I am happy to share my story with you today.

Chapter 1
Innocence Ignited
Early Days and Formative Experiences: Seeds of Empathy and Compassion

It all started in Riverside, California. The year was 1966. We were just your average, everyday, typical American family. Yeah, right—not even typical. There was nothing typical about our family at all. We stuck out like a sore thumb. A typical American family didn't have black gang members hanging out with them almost every other weekend, swimming in our backyard pool, playing Marco Polo, and then enjoying a good old-fashioned American BBQ with hamburgers and hotdogs. The cops would show up because of the so-called concerned neighbors. The neighbors hated us, with the exception of one neighbor and her kids, who we considered family.

Her name was Marguerite, but to us kids, she was known as Auntie Marguerite. She was an awesome cook. Her homemade enchiladas, chile relleno, burritos, homemade tortillas, and tamales were the bomb. She even made bean patties—if you don't know what those are, you're missing out. Auntie Marguerite had talent; that food was damn good. Even her Mexican sweet bread rocked. You know what else rocked about her? She never judged anyone based on the color of their skin.

She judged them by their character the content of their minds. These young men who were hanging out in our backyard did not have flawed characters. They weren't going out in public wearing tons of bling-bling, shaking their hands, and flashing gang signals to other gang members or packing nine-millimeter Glocks and shooting at other people or shooting up neighborhoods. No sir, they respected their neighborhood and neighbors simply because they respected life.

You see, back then, people didn't air their dirty laundry or differences in public. Back then, human beings were respectful of other people's rights. They weren't playing incredibly loud music, talking loudly in coffee shops, letting their kids run amok while others were working, or drag racing down public streets.

Endangering other people's lives was not something we did because of respect. If we felt the urge to do something wildly stupid, we actually drove out into the desert dirt roads to settle our differences, usually due to getting an inflated ego. See the difference? Even our young black American (or, if you prefer, African American) friends knew this.

They had dreams and aspirations, and they wanted to do the right thing with their lives, to make a difference. They weren't out to rob or steal from anybody. And they weren't afraid to work to better themselves either. Martin Luther King Jr. once said the following, which is what would become the most significant quote in American history. It went something like this.

"I have a dream that one day, my children will not be judged by the color of their skin, but by the content of their character (mind)." In other words, the way they think, what they do, their actions, choices, and what kind of parental influences they had growing up. The good Dr. King wasn't talking about controlling his children; he was talking about giving them guidance, direction, and emotional support. In doing these things for his children, he was planting seeds of wisdom. God used him because Dr. King willingly allowed it.

If only people in today's society would just put their iPhones, Android phones, and earbuds away and actually start talking to people again. This society could still have a chance. Everything starts somewhere, and everything has a purpose. However, if we abuse these things, we begin to get addicted to them. What was once a tool becomes an addictive vice. Don't let a piece of electronic equipment control you ever again. You control you. Take back control of your mind. Pray, meditate, watch, listen, and learn. Talk to God, for all the answers come from Him.

Remember this: a child knows nothing of right or wrong. They're innocent. They learn from watching and listening to the people around them—family, friends, relatives, TV, etc. Their learning process actually starts at the first eighteen weeks from conception. It's at this point they can hear the mother's heartbeat.

From six to seven months, they can hear what's going on in the outside world. Are you starting to get the picture now? That unborn baby is going to pick up everything it hears going on outside of the mother. It's going to learn manipulation, love, respect, disrespect, or hate, depending on how the unborn child is influenced.

Remember, if a child knows no right from wrong, it is completely innocent in the eyes of God. We, however, are not, for in the eyes of God, we are accountable for our actions in each and every way. There is only one way to raise our children. Like it or not, your children must be disciplined when they've done something wrong. If we don't discipline our children when it's needed, we are cheating them from the opportunity of learning a very valuable lesson, a lesson that will one day serve them well in making the right decisions versus making the wrong ones.

On April 4th, 1968, Doctor Martin Luther King Jr. was assassinated. For one month, three weeks, and three days, America would be violently shaken to her core. As the grieving for Doctor King continued, the riots and violence were spreading all across America. My mother and father were told by our young black friends to leave California ASAP, as they couldn't protect us from what was coming.

On April 9th, 1968, we officially left California and headed for Tucson, Arizona, where my Uncle Grant and Aunt Joanne lived. On our way to Tucson, I witnessed things like excessive violence, people getting knocked in the head—some things were even more graphic than that. Things no five-year-old boy should ever see. There were multiple families staying at the rest stops. You know those places that you stop at that say "four-hour rest limit," except these people had been there for days, maybe even weeks. They were living there because they were afraid to go back to their homes, in fear for their lives.

Why wouldn't they be? I mean, America had just lost her mind, right? Wrong. The once sleeping giant was officially awakening to the reality of wanting and getting true justice.

They may have gone about it the wrong way, yet in reality, I believe they just wanted to be heard and for true justice to be done. What they failed to realize was they weren't the only race in America that wanted this too. It would take exactly five US Presidents for America to actually truly become what it claimed to be.

The United States of America. For the first time in American history, it seemed to ring true to the American people and the rest of the world that America was, in fact, still the strongest nation on earth. Why? Because she was united. The tide was changing, leaning in the American (taxpayers') favor. We had our problems, but we worked together to conquer them. We found common ground on which each and every one of us could stand on reason to resolve our conflicts and issues with each other.

Then, at the end of the day, we shook one another's hands after a bar fight or school fight. This usually resulted in a friendship or some kind of alliance. If it was an alliance, it was probably due to the fact that the winner of the fight bought two beers for both to drink and toast to their newfound friendship. If it happened in grade school or high school, the winner usually just shook the loser's hand, and from that moment on, they became friends, more often than not, usually best friends.

In today's America, that doesn't happen anymore. Why? It doesn't take a rocket scientist to figure this one out. It just takes two words: common sense. We all need that. America needs that. Look, there's no question about it, America and Americans have screwed up one of the once greatest nations on earth.

When I was a young boy of ten years old, we had just moved from a big city due to a very greedy landlord and a somewhat confused, lost kid who lived in the apartment behind us, trying to show me something they shouldn't have even known or had any knowledge of at such a young age.

My mother must have sensed something was about to happen. You know, Mother's intuition prompted her to go outside looking for me. First, she noticed a table with a blanket over it on the southeast side of the former grocery store that had been converted into two three-bedroom apartments.

She kept calling my name, and fear was building up inside me from the sound of her voice. At first, I didn't answer until she got a little closer to the table and noticed part of my right shoe hanging out. My heart started beating faster and faster. We were very quiet until my mother yanked the blanket off the table! The other kid, who was two years older than me, ran from underneath the table back into her house as my mother grabbed me by my arm from underneath the table. It was as if she instinctively knew what was going to happen before it even happened. My mother was furious with the little girl because she knew something was about to happen. Thank God it didn't, but it did raise questions in my mind. Luckily, because of my strong belief in God, even though I was a young boy, I believed that there was a God and still do today. I was able to deal with it as I got older and was told it wasn't my fault because the girl had apparently been sexually abused by her stepfather.

Now, I know what you're thinking: there are counseling programs for this sort of thing. But this happened in 1969. There were no real counseling programs for kids going through things like that. Nothing like that existed yet. There was nothing you could do about it except go to church, and you didn't talk about it ever again. But being a seven-year-old boy at the time, I had questions. So, I would ask the Catholic priest who was in charge of Our Lady of Perpetual Help Church. I'd ask questions like, "Am I going to hell?"

"Did I do something wrong that made her want to do that? Did I make that happen?"

He realized that I had questions in my mind that were placed there because of doubt, and he assured me, "No, you're not going to hell because you didn't do anything wrong," he explained. "She's like that because she's been sexually abused by her father, which is a mortal sin in God's eyes."

Honestly, I never really understood mortal or venial sins. I mean, sin is sin, right? Anyway, back to my story. Now, where was I? Ah, yes, this is the part where the priest is talking. Sorry about that. "And God will deal with him when the time is right. In His time, not ours.

The fact that you're even asking this shows that this has confused you greatly."

Then I said to him, "But what about the girl? What's going to happen to her?"

He looked me straight in the eye and said, "Pray for her. In time, prayer heals all emotional wounds as well as the physical ones. You see, when someone loses their innocence at a very young age, it can cause damage on all levels: mentally, emotionally, and spiritually."

For a child knows nothing about right from wrong; those characteristics have to be taught to us from the very beginning. If not, it can mess up the child's mind and life. The priest then smiled and said, "Just pray for her. God will take care of her, I promise."

Now, I know what you're thinking: a Catholic priest, really? You must remember this happened in 1969, not in the twenty-first century. My parents realized that we had to move, so we did, to another part of Glendale—same landlord, different neighborhood, with great neighbors who were like family to us. We stayed there for two and a half years. These were some great times for all of us until the greedy landlord physically threatened my dad at an old Safeway Food store located on Glendale Avenue, which is now a thrift store.

He demanded that my father pay the rent immediately. It was two months late due to the fact my father had gotten laid off, and jobs were really hard to get back then. Until he got lucky and landed a job working for Shamrock Foods in the dairy department, making really great money at a great company and still somewhat of a great company today, from what I've heard.

Whoops, I got a little sidetracked there for a moment, or if you prefer, distracted. It was due to the fact that the laws for renting a house were a little more lenient and renter-friendly back then, not to mention the physical assault I witnessed against my father kind of had a hand in it.

The judge gave the landlord a choice: let Mr. Knight and his family stay in the house for five more months and forget about the two months back rent or go to jail for fifteen days plus a $200 fine. The choice is yours. The landlord immediately replied, "But, but, your honor..." He knew if he spent 15 days in jail, he would lose a lot of money.

The judge said, "No buts. That will give him plenty of time to find another place for them to live, and I'll dismiss the assault and battery charge Mr. Knight and the store manager filed against you if that's okay with the plaintiff?"

My dad said, "No problem, your honor, and thank you."

The judge smiled and said, "You're welcome," then saluted him and dismissed the case. We had won a major victory that day.

Five months later, we moved to a then-small town known as Avondale, Arizona. My mom and dad had just bought a brand new house they acquired through a VA loan due to the fact my father was a highly decorated World War II and Korean War veteran with two tours of duty under his belt. He even enlisted in the United States Air Force after the wars.

With all the military training he endured, my father knew how to survive just about any situation that life would throw at him, even the one where my brother Mel had gotten stuck by a medical needle by some deranged kid whose father happened to be a doctor. He found it amusing watching my brother freak out and go into shock.

This happened when he was in the fifth grade in Glendale, Arizona. It messed him up for many years mentally, physically, and spiritually. From that point on, he would be homeschooled until his first year of public school as a freshman in high school.

This was a good thing, or so it seemed. He was adapting well to returning to the public school system until a group of his teenage classmates thought they would have some fun with my older brother by putting him into a cage made for storing students' woodworking class projects. My brother refused to give them the satisfaction of any emotional or physical reaction.

Instead, he just sat there and waited until the teacher, Mr. Turney, returned to his classroom. When Mr. Turney quietly entered the class, he soon punished those students for what they did to Mel. My brother was also Mr. Turney's student assistant, which made the matter even worse. My brother was really quiet even when Mr. Turney opened the cage door. After he opened the door, letting my brother out, the students remained dead quiet. Then the bell rang, and class was over.

These guys thought they were off the hook. No, Mr. Turney quietly went to lock the door with his key, then lined them all up one by one. He bent them over and spanked them really hard with a wooden paddle that had holes drilled through it. You could feel the wind going through it, and you could feel the heat, too, if you know what I mean.

This was the fuel that would continuously feed the fire for the next three years, igniting my brother's drive to change his life. Little did I know that mine would be changing too. Our father died in the summer on July 9th, 1979. My life, my brother's lives, and my sister's life would never be the same. My brother Mel, who pushed me to work out, had just been hired on with Parker, an aerodynamics division that made planes and other equipment for the military. I think they had a contract with Lockheed Martin or Honeywell, I believe.

Anyway, my brother got this really awesome job making really good money. But there was a certain requirement - you have to be 100% healthy to work there. The doctor diagnosed him and it turned out he had really high blood pressure, so they let him go. But they paid him to quit, so all wasn't lost. My brother went to college on a student loan and got a job as a security guard at GCC-Glendale Community College in Glendale, Arizona.

There, he met Captain Ron, and they later became roommates. They studied martial arts under Darryl Khalid. Captain Ron was a martial arts badass trained by Darryl Khalid, who's now a Grand Master and had a dojo off of 59th Avenue and Camelback, right behind the Churches Chicken located there today. My other brother, Don, was busy working at the Revco drug store, and there wasn't anyone around to help me.

I was made to do everything for my mom by myself - you name it, I did it. I felt cheated being the youngest male in the whole family. I had to get a job, go to school full-time, do the yard work, wash the dishes, etc. And work a full-time job. It was hard, but I did it. My uncle sat me down a week after my father died; we had a long heart-to-heart that started with these words, "Son, today is the day you will become a man," boy, he wasn't kidding.

I felt my innocence kind of slipping away with all the things I was learning. Life was getting tougher but more interesting. I realized I could make something of myself. For the first time in my life, I realized, with all the books I read and the research I did as a young boy, that I wasn't doomed to fail. I was destined to fly like an eagle. Success was calling me, and I would eventually answer the call.

You see, we were pretty much still innocent children who struggled with what was right and what was wrong. It was the belief system that our mother and the Catholic Church had put in our heads as young boys which made us this way. It may not have been their intention to do so at the time, unfortunately, that was the end result. Until our minds had broadened and we began to wake up to how it really was. To sum it up in simpler terms, we had learned that life truly isn't fair, especially to men, and we were becoming men.

Unfortunately, my older brother Mel would never be the same after enlisting in the USAF (United States Air Force). All of his issues came back to haunt him so much that he tried to jump out of a window that, if I'm not mistaken, was about seven stories up. He was given an honorable discharge due to extenuating circumstances. Yet, he didn't come home for years after a failed relationship with an enlisted woman he met during basic training before his honorable discharge went through. I believe he always carried a picture of her in his wallet. I don't really think he loved her or she loved him. I knew something had changed in Mel's life based on the way he was holding her picture in church and crying throughout the service. I believe it was just before the New Year on a Sunday morning. I could hear him whispering, "I'm sorry Debra, I'm sorry," over and over again, holding her picture and waiting to get back to the base.

That would be the last time he was told by his CO to gather his gear as he would be going home, as his honorable discharge had come through. He didn't come home, though. Instead, he joined a religious cult, not knowing it at the time.

It wasn't all bad, though, as he would meet his future wife, Lisa Clair Martinson, who is legally known as Lika Knight now. She is a beautiful woman with a beautiful heart and soul. They had two children, a girl and a boy. Their daughter's name is Shalom, and their son's name is David. They are both amazing, loving, caring, and beautiful beings and Christians who understand what the word "repent" truly means. Good job, Mel, good job, Lika.

My relationship with my brother Mel had been strained throughout the years due to the fact that he became jealous of my talents and abilities, as well as my commitment to succeed. According to what my mother told me years ago when my brother listened to his wife and took her advice, they didn't fully understand how the workman's comp insurance process actually worked.

We humans are only afraid of the unknown. Apparently, my brother either forgot that or never learned it. If only they had called me and asked, that whole mess could have been avoided. It was the first workman's comp insurance letter my brother had ever received. All of the first letters start out like this: "At this time, your claim is being denied." Now, here's what my brother did instead of calling me or someone who knows about workman's comp laws. He decided, with the advice of his loving wife, to go down to the Kmart store where he was employed at the time, show that HR official who's boss, and demand they pay the claim. Well, it didn't work. All he succeeded in doing was scaring the heck out of a little four-foot-eleven-inch, one-hundred-pound woman to the point where she felt like she was going to get hurt really, really bad. This made the situation ten times worse, as there was now a warrant out for my brother's arrest.

That put him and their family in a very bad financial situation, causing Mel not to be able to get any more gainful employment to provide for his family until our Mother stepped in and begged me to help him.

Which I did, four days later, I would live to regret it. I fixed his life while he unknowingly had destroyed mine. Don't get me wrong, I love my brother and still love him dearly.

I often think of how he pushed me to the limit to better myself by teaching me to stand up for my rights. Thank you, brother, for being there at a moment in time when I truly needed some guidance and motivation to push me over the edge. This caused me to have to confront my fears and persevere to succeed in the goals that we presented to one another by getting physically fit and stronger and watching my body change overnight. Thank you, brother, for being there when I needed you most. I love you, Mel.

After all that, something was happening inside me. I felt like I was losing my reason for being. Nothing seemed to make sense anymore; everything I touched, everything I had planned seemed like it was falling apart—it was. I was angry with myself for allowing myself to be manipulated by my flesh and blood, by my mother. I couldn't believe this was happening to me.

How could my very own flesh and blood betray my good nature, betray me, then turn around and literally stab me in the back and smile while they put the knife in my back—unbelievable.

I could not believe my luck. Well, human beings will do that, especially my family. Jealousy, envy, and strife are very ugly things and they do exist. It's up to us to control those things with the help of God, and not let them get out of control. But what hurt the most was that my mom did it to me again, just like she did with my oldest brother Mark; she denied that she begged me to get my brother Mel a job, and I told her that, which she continuously denied that she begged me to give him a job. I kept telling her she did say that, which she did. She'd denied it and got very angry every time I repeatedly mentioned it.

It was official, I would soon be at war with my entire family for doing the right thing. I was taught to love, honor, and respect my family, friends, relatives, even strangers. I was taught to treat others the way I want to be treated. Unfortunately, it wasn't my family that taught me that; it was a human relations/home-economics teacher by the name of Debra or Debbie Beard, who later became Mrs. Shalensic, I believe.

She was great, and I felt safe opening up to her. I was her student assistant in home economics and human relations during my Junior and Senior year of high school. She even said that after meeting my mom and brother, she could sense I was afraid or scared to death because my mom was pushing Donald's emotional buttons, my other brother Mel's twin. She even tried to talk to my mother, who obviously wasn't herself anymore, and had become addicted to Ativan, which some quack psychiatrist prescribed.

And I do mean quack; he was investigated later on for sexual assault among other things involving other female patients.

This drug really changed her; she hated me with a passion when she was taking it. Out of all her kids, and I don't know why, to this day, I don't know why. She even tried to beat me to death with a steel pipe after she found a Playboy magazine in my room, and kept calling me a little imp. Lucky for me, Mel intervened and took the pipe away from her just in time; she had succeeded in unknowingly busting open the top right side of the back of my head. I believe it was the Ativan that made her act this way. Hell, she even said I deserved to die.

Seriously, really, I was a confused, frightened teenager going through that changing period in my life, you know, adolescence. My male hormones were in overdrive. Nobody even talked to me about anything; my other brothers got the talk, though from our oldest brother. My male hormones were in overdrive.

I would have to figure it out all on my own; indirectly, Playboy helped me. I wasn't an imp; my body was changing. I wasn't evil. I was becoming a young man. I don't think my mom really ever comprehended the damage she did that day when she called me the devil's child, which would continuously haunt me up until I was in my mid-20s.

Even after all that hell she put me through, I still loved her and wanted to give her a better life. She would have had all that and more if she just would have listened to me. I was planning on buying her a house away from all the bullshit going on in the neighborhood she still called home. It wasn't home anymore; it had become a gang war zone, which was obvious when I moved back to Arizona from Dallas, Texas. That was the first thing I noticed.

Funny thing, though, I was actually excited when I first moved back there to see my mother, relatives, and friends - at least, I thought they were my friends. Let's just say that the Italians knew exactly what they were talking about when they say, "Keep your friends close but your enemies closer." Yep, they knew!

It's a shame that I couldn't actually exercise that because of all the people who were turning against me. Left with no alliances of my own, or people who had my back - those people were back in Texas. Yep, I was alone, completely alone, for the first time in my life. If only I had listened to my ex-wife, who had warned me not to go back there, maybe, just maybe, my life would have been different. Unfortunately, it would take many years for that to happen, many, many years.

I had learned a very valuable lesson through all of this - our destiny is defined by the choices we make. In the end, it's not really what you accomplish in life that counts. It's how you live it that counts. By you just living being alive, there's not only power in that, there's purpose. In other words, by simply living and being somewhere along in your life, you made choices that affected others on your life path in both positive and negative ways.

A child needs to be able to learn from their mistakes in order to grow. A child also needs to play outside to energize their bodies and minds in order for them to become productive, producing adults, which the world so desperately needs right now. Children today are left alone with a big-screen TV if their parents can afford one, or a computer screen; which can give them access to almost anything they can type out on the keyboard. They eat a ton of fast foods, aka junk foods. Lounging around the house getting fat, or obese if you prefer, but I'm not going to sugarcoat it.

This isn't good for the children or the parents. It's because of these electronic babysitters that our children are losing their innocence at a very young age. For a child knows nothing of right or wrong until they're taught it, the problem is they're not being taught by their parents. They're being taught by computers, public schools, and online video games, etc.

Don't let this continue to happen; take the initiative and time to show them exactly how much they mean to you by starting to listen to them - I mean really listen to them. And for God's sakes, put the phone away when you're talking to them; give them your complete and undivided attention.

God gave them to you for a reason - to love and protect, honor, discipline, to shepherd them when it's needed. This will eventually mold them into productive human beings and not out-of-control adults who think they know it all. Protecting them and their innocence will make a difference not only in their lives but also in others.

It made a difference in my life by finding someone who truly cared whether I lived or died, and how I lived. Just knowing that was all I needed to become a productive, loving, caring human being. We're all here for a reason; we all have a purpose for being. It's up to us to find and nurture that purpose. In doing so, the world will become a more loving, caring, compassionate, and productive place. A child's innocence is a very precious gift given to them by God. It's up to the parents to make sure they keep it for a very long time. Protect your children, discipline them when they need discipline. Don't be their buddy - they're not your buddy; they are gifts of life entrusted to you from God. Respect that fact, then watch what happens as they transition into men and women who know real love, understanding, and compassion for their fellow mankind. You'll feel a tremendously powerful sense of accomplishment knowing you were used as a conduit to get them to where they are. Isn't that beautiful to realize that? Isn't that really what being a good parent actually is?

Chapter 2
The Spark of Action
First Steps into a Larger World Discovering the Impact of Small Acts

When I was a young boy of eleven years old, I would open doors for women and children. Yes, chivalry was alive and well then. We were taught right from wrong, and the people back then would laugh and joke around with each other without getting all butt hurt. We didn't wear our emotions on our sleeves, and we were never easily offended by what some people would say or do. There was a really popular saying we pretty much stuck to that we used as a catalyst to shut down the bullies. It goes something like this: "Sticks and stones may break my bones, but names will never hurt me." Words can't hurt you. They're just words - they have no power over you if you ignore them. What has happened to this generation that has chosen to allow name-calling to be an emotional button pusher? If nobody physically assaults you, just walk away. But never, ever turn your back when you do. A coward will always take that as a sign of weakness. As you walk away, always maintain eye contact and silence. And always maintain visual observation of them to avoid any unexpected surprises.

We are all human beings learning each and every day. Hopefully, we are experiencing life to the fullest by contributing to humanity's or humankind's very existence, if you prefer. As a young boy, I was really into reading the Bible and self-help books - obviously not your everyday average American kid.

The passages and books in the Bible were and still are very entertaining and knowledgeable to me, especially this verse about tithing: (Leviticus 27:30, The tithe is introduced into law) "A tenth of everything from the land, whether grain from the soil or fruit from the trees, belongs to the LORD; it is holy to the LORD."

As I watched my brother Donald, the third oldest, Mel's identical twin, who became one of the Church's regular Ushers collecting tithes, I had questions - life-changing questions like if we're supposed to give ten percent of everything we own (wages of our labor, work) to the LORD aka God, what is our true purpose for being, why are we here.

After reading the book *Think and Grow Rich,* I finally understood why tithing was necessary. It helped to contribute to the poor, the good of the community, so they could feed their families and give thanks to God. Somewhere in today's society, that message has become blurred by the greed of the churches and religious congregations. You see, as a young boy who had witnessed the cons, con men, and con artists trying to hustle my family while growing up in Avondale, Arizona.

Somehow, I had always sensed when someone was trying to hustle us. I would tell my mother and siblings not to be so freely giving to these people. "They won't do it for you when the tables are turned," I'd say. My mother would always respond, "You don't know that to be true. Stop saying it. They're our neighbors and friends."

Years later, she began to realize I had been right in more ways than one. We had a plethora of using neighbors and so-called friends. My family couldn't see it, but I could. So, I adapted my own philosophy regarding our so-called neighbors: "Don't do it for them; they're not going to help you when you need it the most." It turned out I was right on all counts.

Our neighbors were leeches, users, and manipulators who couldn't manipulate me, yet they were able to do it to my family members. Why? I believe it was because of what I learned from reading the Bible and all the self-help books I read since I was ten years old. It all started with God's word, though—the Bible.

"Seek ye first the Kingdom of God, and all these things will be added unto you." All of God's principles and wisdom were staring me right in the face. Practically every single self-help book I ever read as a young boy and young man, and now as a fully grown man, contained these principles. I had figured out the secret of living a fuller, more meaningful life.

My life was starting to change for the better as the sparks of wisdom flowed through me. My life would never be the same. Everything I touched turned to gold. I had money in the credit union—a lot of money— through my job at Alpha Beta Foods, which later became ABCO Foods. I even bought my own condo and a nice sports car. Yep, I was on top of the world. Nothing could stop me now, or so I thought.

The next seven years would lead me to my true destiny as my life would change overnight—or at least that's what it felt like. Every bit of knowledge I consumed was like a survivor in the desert looking for water, realizing that if he didn't find it, he would die. We must have water just like we must have the knowledge to find it. We must all thirst for knowledge to better ourselves spiritually, mentally, financially, and emotionally.

I was thirsting for more and more knowledge every single day, from the time I woke up in the morning to the time I went to sleep. I did this religiously for six months straight. A fire had been ignited in my soul. I could feel my whole life changing. Did I finally understand God's formulas for spiritual, emotional, and financial success in my life? Did I finally crack the code, or was it just something I wanted to believe that made it real to me?

Only time would tell. I was beginning to put all the pieces of the puzzle together. It was almost magical how it was starting to become simple knowledge to me. Why? Because God doesn't make life complicated—we do. He shows us that we need simplicity in our lives more than we'd like to admit. Once we're ready to admit this to ourselves and ask for God's help—aka our Creator, Jesus, Joshua—we become unstoppable. With God included in our lives, we'll grow wiser in how to live a more fruitful, enriching life. All we have to do is ask, and have faith, and it will be given.

There's only one catch: God wants our attention. Are you LISTENING? In a television show where a well-known actor plays a famous radio psychiatrist, his favorite saying was, "I'm listening." His character realized that if he let people know he was truly listening, he would shut up and let them talk until they were done. Then, they would sit down, shut up, and hear what he had to say. Based on his response, they could tell if he was truly listening.

Would our lives make more sense and be more meaningful if we only took the time to really listen to others who are going through rough patches in their lives? You bet they would. Life is about give and take. When two people come together and consciously decide to really listen to one another, something marvelous happens. They both get something in return—that's called give and take, the way I believe our Divine Creator intended us to act. In so doing, a personal bond, an alliance, can usually be formed between the two individuals.

I'll give you a classic example. Mr. Eldritch, the guy whose lawn I used to mow for $4.00 every other week when we lived in Glendale, Arizona, off of Maryland Avenue, taught me about business. He gave me an education free of charge. When he talked, I would shut up and listen. I didn't interrupt him. I learned to listen between the lines and, in return, I got some valuable information because I was an effective listener at such a very young age. I was seven years old when I met him. He taught me about business, rapport, and money, and he told me to get the book *Think and Grow Rich.*

It was a Friday night. My mom and dad had just taken us all out for Smitty's pizza—it was the best. Then, on the way home, they stopped at Thrifty Food and Drugs. Thrifty was a really cool place. They had the best ice cream and really cool products—stereos, radios, and books. I loved books and still do today, especially this one, *Think and Grow Rich* the one Mr. Eldritch told me about. It was now in my hands as I walked towards my mom and dad, beaming with confidence. I made a deal with my mom and dad to buy me the book as I explained to them how badly I needed that book and how they could take it out of my $ 2.00-a-week allowance for the next three weeks. The year was 1969, and $2.00 a week could buy a lot back then, but it wasn't enough to buy the book. I really wanted that book. My mom and dad agreed to my terms. It was the most powerful book I ever read. It really opened my eyes, thank you, Napoleon Hill, for writing it. It changed my way of thinking and also changed my life.

The wheels kept turning. The fire was burning fever-ishly inside me. I wanted to learn, and I wanted to grow. I wanted to take in as much knowledge as I possibly could and learn trades and become an investor, just like Napoleon Hill talked about investing in yourself in his book and always remaining persistent. I was ready; nothing was going to stop me, nothing.

It would be exactly one year after my father died, and I had become a real man at the age of sixteen. I was no longer working out with my brother Mel anymore. He had started going to GCC, Glendale Community College. I still kept working out, though, so did he. I was pretty much following in my brother's footsteps. I would always watch him bagging groceries when he worked for A.J. Bayless Foods as a Courtesy Clerk. That was my training ground.

Now, I was working there as a Courtesy Clerk six months later after my brother quit. John Welch, my brother's former boss, asked me this question when I applied for the job before he hired me, "Think you're as good as your brother?"

If my memory serves me correctly, I believe this was my reply: "In our family, the apple doesn't fall too far from the tree."

He extended his hand, and we shook hands. He looked me in the eye and said, "Congratulations, you're hired. When can you start?"

I said, "Today, if you need me." I ran home, took a quick shower, changed out of my school clothes, put on a shirt and tie, black slacks, etc.

I know what you're thinking. The hiring process doesn't move that quickly. Well, guess what, back then it did. We didn't have all the red tape, restrictions that we have today. There was no need for it back then. A person's word of honor actually meant something back then. People were honorable, respectful, and even humble. We weren't like lost homeless puppies running around the streets looking for our next meal or place to sleep. We practiced God's teachings on a consistent basis.

We went out with family and friends, we had fun, going out with no fears or anxiety whatsoever. Doesn't the Bible say in Ecclesiastes 3:4-5, "A time to weep, a time to laugh; A time to mourn and a time to dance. A time to throw away stones and a time to gather stones; A time to embrace and a time to refrain from embracing." There's more to this, but you get the idea, in other words, simply put, there's a time for everything. If we just learn to keep it simple, let go of the wheel, relax, and let God take the wheel and watch what happens. Now I'm not saying to just relax and sit on your ass. You have to get up and move, you gotta allow things to gracefully happen. It's all part of God's process and promise to us. For true faith without works is dead.

I just recalled an old joke that my father, I believe, once shared with us when I was younger. We were all gathered around the fire in the backyard, roasting marshmallows, laughing and having a good time. Then my dad started telling this joke about this Christian who was stuck on a sinking boat. A small boat came by and asked him if he needed any help. He said, "No, thank you, I'm praying to My Lord for the right time to leave this sinking ship."

About twenty minutes later, another ship came around him. Again, they asked him if he needed any help. Again his reply was this! "No, thank you. I'm waiting for the right time for My Lord God to send me a messenger to rescue me." Now, the boat had sunk so low that he was standing on the bow of the boat.

This time it would be thirty minutes before a luxury cruise ship showed up. "Ahoy, do you need any help?"

Again, his reply was the same. "No, thank you, I'm waiting for My Lord God to send me one of his messengers to rescue me."

Well, his boat ended up sinking, he drowned and died, then went to heaven, Jesus welcomed him with open arms. The Christian man looked around, at first he thought he was dreaming. But when Jesus hugged him, he realized he was in heaven. Jesus said, "Welcome my son." The man still wondering why The Lord didn't deliver him from drowning on a sinking ship. Asked him the following question:

"Lord, you said that once I decided to follow you, you'd protect and keep me in your grace, yet when I needed you the most in my hour of need you didn't send me any help."

The Lord put his right hand on the man's left shoulder and said this. "You idiot, I sent you three messengers." The moral of the story is simple, don't wait for something to happen, take action and truly listen to the voice of reason. Get off the fence and take action today.

I was always a risk-taker, even at a young age. Some risks maybe should have been avoided altogether as the price would become too high to pay emotionally and sometimes even financially. Here is a perfect example of one such incident of which the stakes were very high. I heard my mother say religiously from the age of ten to my teen years up until my father died.

It would be these words that tricked me and trapped me emotionally into believing that I could be the one guy on the planet who would save the female populace from ever being taken advantage of or used in any way, shape, or form, sexually, financially, or emotionally ever again. All men want is one thing from a woman, and that's sex. At that very moment, she may not have realized it, but she planted a seed.

That seed was to save the neglected, used and abused female populace. After five years of hearing her say this every time she and my father were fighting, she would say this to me after she threw out my dad numerous times. She often would look at me and say these words. "You're going to grow up just like your father and older brother Marcus. All men want from a woman is one thing - sex." Well, she didn't know it at the time, but she had indirectly altered my future. From that moment on, I would become a White Knight, living with only one purpose - to prove to all women, especially the ones I was attracted to, that I was different.

I would become their Knight in shining armor, waiting to rescue them from all the bad things that were happening in their lives because of men. Don't get me wrong here, for there is and was such a thing as a damsel in distress. And more often than not, a lot of those were legit, but when you tell your son who's very impressionable, who's only ten years old for five years straight that all men want is sex. What do you think is going to happen to him when he becomes a full-grown man?

Yep, you guessed it! He's going to develop a rescue syndrome, also known as The White Knight Syndrome. Yep, there's power in words, be careful of what you say for our tongues are like a double-edged sword that cuts both ways, in creating or granting life or death. Now life can have many meanings, such as the bearer of fruit which means to blossom and grow. Or we have death, which means to wither away, to no longer be, to return to the ashes to ashes, dust to dust.

Even with our words, as you can see, there's power over life and death. Not necessarily so much in dying, it's more like what you're saying that's either going to cause a person to grow and bear positive fruits of their labors. Or the negative things that indirectly will lead them on a path of self-destruction, hopefully they will see it, and wake up someday with professional help, love, compassion, and understanding to getting them to the point of leading a blessed and meaningful life. I mean isn't that why we're here, to learn and find our purpose?

What would you do if you woke up tomorrow, and everything and everyone you ever cared about was gone? Life is a gift, we are all living in the physical moment right now. Don't ever take it for granted, you're here, we're all here for a reason. Find your purpose, make a difference in someone's life today. Become a man of nobility and valor. Witness lives being changed just by setting an example. Start talking to people, human beings are social creatures, that's no accident.

We're created in the image of our divine creator, that's no accident. Here's a question for all of us to think about! What if we signed a contract to come here and experience this life? Right before we signed, we were shown what it would be like, the choices we'd make in advance. We more than likely would have responded like this, piece of cake. Except, there's one catch right after we signed it. We were told one more thing. The catch was, after we were born into this world, we wouldn't remember a thing.

Now, if this is true, and this actually happened, then maybe, just maybe it was either a trick to get us here, an experiment of some sort. Or it will make for one hell of a great movie one day. Hmmm, that's definitely something to consider down the road, maybe in later years. Anyway, I think by now you probably get the picture here, right? Life is what we make it.

People used to like to go to the movies to forget; it was a form of escape for them. Watching the Leading Men and Leading Ladies on the silver screen perform, if they decided at any time throughout the movie to go to the snack bar and get pop and popcorn, the actors failed to hook their audience. The BS, aka bullshit meter, immediately went off. And the illusion failed.

There was an almost completely unknown actor who was quite good, who got interviewed on Entertainment Tonight. He was asked this question, "How do you do it Bruce?"

He replied, "I come from a dysfunctional background. Dysfunctional people make the best actors because they can relate to practically any situation the director throws them into. They're special people who were forced to deal with extenuating circumstances."

When you stop to think about it, you begin to realize that everything happens for a reason. There are no accidents in life. The Late Great Adam Roarke (My

Mentor) used to always say this. "What happened was supposed to happen. The question is, why does it keep happening over and over again?" Think about that for a second, concentrate on the outcome that you want, then watch what happens.

Are you starting to see a pattern here? If you're not beginning to notice the pattern, I can sum it up for you in three words. You didn't learn. In other words, like Albert Einstein once said, "The definition of insanity is doing the same thing over and over again and expecting different results." Therefore, there truly are no accidents in life; everything is happening for a reason. The reason is, you didn't learn.

A mistake isn't really a mistake; indirectly it is an opportunity to learn when you think about it. No, really, that's exactly what it is. A true lesson learned is not a mistake. It's a learning process that actually helps us best when we watch, listen, and learn. The world today has gotten so screwed up because of technology abuse. It seems like the whole world is under some kind of hypnotic worldwide web spell. We're trapped in a virtual matrix every single day we wake up from bed.

Now you're probably thinking, what is the point of all of this? The point is simple, just like Gandhi once said,

"You must be the change you wish to see in the world." At the time he said this, the world needed to hear it, as mankind was heading into a very dark and sinister time. Gandhi's words caused most of humanity to take a long, deep look into the future.

By the way, Gandhi was a Civil Rights Lawyer, anti-colonial nationalist, an author, and political ethicist who employed nonviolent resistance to lead a successful campaign for India's independence from British rule. He inspired movements for civil rights and freedom all across the world.

He was assassinated on January 30, 1948. Gandhi was a man who died fighting for what he believed in. Everything he did started out small, eventually becoming significant in all of our lives. All things happen for a reason; it's up to us to find that reason, as there are no accidents. One man can make a difference. Don't let the government or the media dictate to you or anyone else that you can't make a difference.

All the great teachers throughout history — Jesus Christ, Buddha, Gandhi, President Kennedy, Moses, Mother Teresa, Albert Einstein, and Nikola Tesla — taught us this. They all had one thing in common. They believed that love conquers all. Look at the state of the world today. It saddens me to see the current condition of this now selfish, take, take world today.

With the attitude of "what can you do for me" versus "how can we make a positive difference in this world," when material things and status become more important than helping one another, humanity loses. Material things are only temporary; a legacy will last forever. We all have an inherent responsibility to lead our youth, the younger generation, in the right direction even if it means sometimes giving them a good swift kick in the butt.

Now, I'm not talking about actually kicking them. I'm talking about getting their attention, getting and keeping them motivated to find their true purpose. Each generation that has followed the other generations from the fifties to the late eighties used to do this. There's always someone willing to help you do this. I pray that the right people will find you; they're out there, trust me on this. They will find you; you just have to specifically ask for them when you pray.

If you want to really change your life, you have to change your thinking, and you must develop good habits. Stop going out to the clubs, chasing girls, and wasting your money and time. Don't let your hormones dictate your future. I've met way too many young men who are always talking about baby mama drama. Many young men who had so much potential literally screw their lives up being in these kinds of situations. It's not worth it.

Instead of letting your body train you, you train your body. Never underestimate the power of your mind; it can break you or make you. It's your choice; choose wisely, don't become a statistic. And always be learning, it's your body, your mind, what will you decide.

Did you know that an Olympic Athlete trains approximately three to four hours a day. Why, to build up their strength, endurance, speed, and most importantly focus. Do you think if they went out to the club every weekend or two to three times a week, they could achieve this? No, it's not going to happen, simply because they're lacking the one most important ingredient to become a true champion, focus. Without focus, nothing will happen.

What do you think would happen if the men who became Knights in the thirteenth century never trained or honed their skills, perfected them? Well, they would have died. Sir John Chandos was a young man who rose from an obscure poor family. He later became the hero of the Hundred Years War, a knight distinct from all the others. This means he stood out. How did he do that? Through vigorous intense military training, he refused to become a slave to obscurity. Instead, he chose to be the master of his destiny by preparing for his journey.

People today are constantly being bombarded with ads on the internet and trying to do two or three things at one time. This creates mass confusion which renders our brains not able to adapt to multiple information. This can become very dangerous to all humanity, it can even affect your mind as you grow older, causing a self-inflicted disease known as Alzheimer's, or worse, dementia at a very young age. A disciplined mind will continue to serve you all your life. An undisciplined mind will not.

Yes, we have become entangled in a web, the world wide web. That's slowly but surely taking possession of us all because we've become or are becoming complacent. If we don't get back to not being comfortable, it's a pretty fair bet we'll become so complacent that we will eventually do nothing for ourselves, loved ones, friends, etc. It's true a computer is capable of doing multiple things at one time. But, is it also not true that a computer when something isn't right, it will shut itself down?

If a human being built the computer! Which they did! Doesn't that make it vulnerable in some way, shape, or form? You better believe it does. Is it not possible that those very same vulnerabilities can also cause malfunctions that could cause a possible butterfly effect that could potentially lead to humanity's end.

We have a moral obligation to all humanity to be of service to others. We need to take a few steps back, learn from our ancestors' experiences, find a common ground that we can all stand firm on. To re-establish the connection (human connection) we are not machines. We are human beings capable of amazing things. These electronic devices will either serve us, or we will end up serving them. I myself prefer they serve me.

Using them for the good of humanity will also result in a loving, caring, respectful society. After all, isn't that what we all really want. Chasing money, fame, and fortune is a sucker's bet. Don't let yourself become seduced by its beckoning snare, waiting for you to take the bait, draining your soul. Leaving you with nothing but shattered dreams of what could have been. Go outside, take a walk, bask in the sun that God created for all living things.

Let it fully recharge your body, bring it back to life. Don't listen to the naysayers, do the opposite of what they're doing. Watch how your body responds as you become more aware of everything around you. My grandmother used to say to me, take time to stop and smell the roses. It's time to stop and smell the roses. Time to live life to the fullest, get off the phones, turn off all the distractions and live to your fullest potential. A distracted society is a dangerous society. I give a great example of what I'm talking about here.

How safe is it to drive your vehicle nowadays? People don't seem to give a rat's ass about the other drivers on the road, period. I mean, what the hell is happening to America? We have selfish younger people texting and driving, swerving into other drivers' lanes. Hello, put the phone down and concentrate on the road. I had too many close calls because of these willfully ignorant people who don't respect the other drivers who are obeying the traffic laws and paying a hundred percent attention to the road.

News flash for all the willfully ignorant selfish drivers out there. It's because of drivers like me that care about other people's right to live that you are probably still alive. Now, what do you think is going to happen when my generation is no longer around? Honestly, I don't think your generation will make it, if it continues to have its self-righteous, know-it-all attitude. Never learning from its mistakes, keep doing the same crazy messed-up things. Because they think they're superior in some way.

Here's a wake-up call to those out there who don't respect life. Karma is a real bitch when you're playing with other people's lives, and she's coming for you when you least expect it. To avoid her wrath, do unto others as you would have them do unto you. In other words, treat people the way you want to be treated. Respect the road and your fellow drivers. When the light turns green, that means go. It surely doesn't mean sit there and text or surf the internet. Don't be an ass, leave the phone alone - it can save lives, maybe even your own.

In a video game, if you don't like the end result, you just hit the reset button. In real life, you can't do that. You can, however, change the channel, change your course of direction by changing your frequency. How do you do that? By changing the way you think. If you change your thoughts, the possibilities are endless.

Chapter 3
Trials and Tribulations
Confronting Challenges and Adversity:
Lessons in Resilience and Determination

As a young boy, I had many hurdles to jump over. Life had become more demanding and challenging for me. In the public school system, I was always getting bullied - both physically and emotionally put down to the point where I started to shut down emotionally, almost appearing to be invisible.

I reasoned that if they couldn't hear me, they would leave me alone. Unfortunately, I found out that just wasn't true. Instead of getting better, it just got worse - much worse. How much worse, you ask? I was kicked in my stomach and ribs, had the hair on my head pulled, and was ordered to bark like a dog with a circle of emotionally messed up kids around me with a lot of anger and hate issues. This was just one of many incidents that transpired.

Yet, no matter what happened to me at Lattie Coor School, I refused to break. My love for God, my will, and drive couldn't be broken, no matter what. I had become like a rock - no one or anything was going to be able to take me down in any way, shape, or form.

It was two months until summer vacation in 1975. The physical and emotional abuse continued. My dad had started to notice the change in my mental and emotional state, and he decided that enough was enough. On the day when it was time for him to pick me up from school, he showed up about a half-hour early. What my dad witnessed was something so degrading for any child to have to endure.

My sixth-grade teacher, Mrs. Jackson, was a very sick and twisted person. She believed that two white children, the only two in her class, should be goaded into fighting with each other. Just before the end of class, if we didn't fight one another, we would both be forced into a dark cupboard and locked in until it was time to go home. They would laugh and make fun of me and Wayne, calling us stupid white boys and white trash fighting one another.

It was entertainment for her and the other children of color. Oh, by the way, did I mention that my teacher was a black woman? Or, if you prefer, African American - a very sick African American at that. She was made to answer for her crimes of messing with my mind as well as the other so-called white child in her class.

She answered alright, yet nothing really happened to her. She remained a teacher, was questioned about her actions, and that was it. End of the story. This was not only child abuse, it was pure hate. Why wasn't she fired after that? For a season, it ended though after we hired a lawyer, the best lawyer in the state of Arizona at the time (Harry Craig), to investigate and get my brother out of jail for defending me, his baby brother's rights. Finally, justice was served, or was it?

Avondale was obviously corrupt to the core after we filed a lawsuit against Lattie Coor School and the City of Avondale. According to what Harry Craig, our lawyer, said after going to court and defending my brother in the Avondale Court - which Harry called a Kangaroo Court - due to the fact that he knew we would lose on their playing field, until he filed for an appeal to hear the case in Superior Court, in Downtown Phoenix.

Arizona's Superior Court, aka Harry's (our lawyer's) playing field. Guess what? Harry was right - my brother's case was dismissed, and he was free to go. Harry had leveled the playing field. Now it gets really nasty and very, very dirty. After our court victory, the City of Avondale stole our perfectly good, running 1968 Oldsmobile Delta 88. That was one bad-ass powerful car - it was built like a tank too.

It was cream-colored with a tan vinyl top, with almond-colored leather interior. That car was beautiful from all angles. They stole it right out from under our noses, bragging about how the Knight family needed to learn a lesson, and how we didn't know who the hell we were messing with. That car was solid, it ran excellent. Sure, they tagged it, saying it was an inoperative vehicle (they had to make it look good, you know), but it wasn't. She purred like a kitten, meaning she ran strong.

We drove it all over Avondale, Goodyear, Glendale, Peoria, even Phoenix. Everybody witnessed it, yet the City still towed it away. Big mistake; Our Lawyer's legal teeth we're starting to show big-time.

The tides were turning in our favor; everything was starting to come together, even the School was scared and they rightfully should have been. Because they failed me and my family in many, many ways, and they knew it. Not only did I go through unspeakable abuse and pure hell in the school. On top of that, they were all in on it, working together to destroy our good name and reputation. Why they harbored such hatred and contempt against me and my family to this day, I do not know.

They even pulled APS into the equation (Arizona Public Service) by making up a fake amount for an electric bill we couldn't pay, or for that matter, anyone could pay back then. I saw the bill; it said we owed APS eleven hundred and some dollars and cents. Yeah right, it was all made up to look legal, it was complete bull crap. They even tried the same thing with our water.

That's when Harry Craig, our attorney, stepped in. He finally said enough is enough; he threatened to go to the media and tell the whole story if the city didn't turn the water back on right away. Oh, by the way, did I mention this was in the summer? Yeah, can you imagine no water in the summer in Arizona? It was fun, not really though, just trying to put a nice spin on a very nasty and ugly former situation.

As I left Lattie Coor School that year, I breathed a sigh of relief. We had fun that Summer; it was filled with adventure, swimming, Marco Polo, continuous barbecues, homemade ice cream, and hide and seek, even some red light, green light. We even went to the Phoenix Zoo three times that Summer; we were grateful for all the blessings God laid before us at a very dark time in all our lives.

I remember going to the Avondale Junior High School the following year, smelling like smoke from our hooded fireplace my dad and oldest brother Mark installed to keep us warm from the winter cold. It worked with one drawback though, as the black soot was visibly coming out of my ears and my nose from our hooded fireplace, which we had to use during the winter months. Sometimes I would catch my teachers staring at my ears and nostrils, where the black soot was the most noticeable.

They never said anything about it, even though the whole town knew we didn't have any electricity, they acted like they didn't know anything. Back then, people were real busybodies, really minded their own business most of the time, at least that's what they wanted their neighbors and friends to think. And now we unfortunately have a completely new electronic age busybodies who don't even gather all the facts.

After they have done irreparable damage to someone's reputation, this is also called defamation of character, which legally makes them financially accountable for all the damage they caused someone. Legally, if they're taken to court for their reckless actions, the court can make them pay you up to ten times the damages you incurred. Don't believe me, look it up for yourself at your local Law Library.

After my first year in Junior high school, and a few rough patches with some of my seventh-grade peers who continued to verbally and physically abuse me until Ruby, a very beautiful young girl who I had a crush on (I think she knew it), found out I had some hidden talents. I won't go into all of those right now, but I will tell you this; there's one talent I had and still have to this day - singing!

Ruby found out I could sing. She and two other girls somehow convinced the teacher to let me sing in front of the class; the song was "Rhinestone Cowboy" by Glen Campbell. They were all blown away by my performance, even my teacher, Mr. Lindenburg, was blown away.

I had finally achieved the one thing I thought would never happen; in that very moment, I was finally accepted and respected for my talents and abilities, and they could see that I was no different than them, except I had this gift. And life got a little easier, or so it seemed. Even my good friend and neighbor Danny Roderick was blown away; he never said anything about it, though he just started treating me like one of the guys, which until that point he never really did.

I have so much respect and brotherly love for him to this day for all the things he did to help my mother after I moved to Texas to make my last attempt at saving my relationship with my ex-wife, before I officially left her for good as the relationship had become unsalvageable.

It was becoming more and more obvious she was jealous that my star was beginning to rise in Dallas. Others noticed her attempts of trying to sabotage me; she tried to spin it, but it didn't work. She had finally been exposed; no one believed her lies anymore after that.

Even my mentor, Adam Roarke, knew it, as it affected my performances in front of the camera.

After officially meeting Adam Roarke, I continued studying and learning at The Film Actors Lab for almost three years in Las Colinas, Texas. The man was an incredible acting teacher, mentor, and father. He was my mentor and friend who knew exactly how to coach me and sharpen my instincts. News flash for all the wannabe actors out there; ninety percent of acting is technique, and ten percent is talent. Always rely on your instincts to deliver quality work. If the camera doesn't love you, it's not going to work.

Oh, I almost forgot about my good friend Danny Roderick. Much love and respect to you for doing everything you did when I wasn't around to help my mom. Thank you, my friend and brother, for all the limo rides; you made her feel like a queen. According to what my mom used to tell me, you treated her like a queen as well. I'll never forget what you did. Rest in Peace, brother. Danny passed away back on September 11th, 2021. You are definitely missed, my friend. Godspeed to you, brother. Godspeed.

Danny and I became really good friends when my father died in July of 1979. Life hit my entire family really hard then. On the day he died, the county hospital was pretty much telling him that his wife was very sick and should be admitted immediately into the county hospital. Mom hated the county hospital.

My dad died having an argument with the doctor about that very thing and accidentally slugged a nurse in the face as his body gave out. He fell face down as he hit the floor; they found out (The doctors) he had multiple heart attacks before, he just never said anything. He died of an aneurysm. This happened after he came home from paying his last respects to his mother who had recently died in Pennsylvania.

Exactly three weeks after flying back home to Arizona, my father died. Two weeks after he passed away, and after a very long heartfelt talk from my Uncle Buddy, an avid antique car collector, engineer I believe, gold connoisseur entrepreneur (haha, no seriously he was), I would become the man of the house. That meant going to school, holding down a full-time job, and graduating high school. Now, keep in mind I was just a fifteen-year-old teenager trying to find my way in life two weeks ago, who now unexpectedly became a man overnight.

As I was just beginning to figure out life, all of a sudden from out of nowhere, I had the weight of the world thrown on my shoulders. Wow, but I didn't let it beat me down. Instead, I adapted, I innovated, and I overcame. I didn't let it break me; I let it make me.

I pulled out the book that I bought when I was a young boy, Napoleon Hill's *Think and Grow Rich*. Got a job working at AJ Bayless Market as a courtesy clerk, aka bagger, the most well-known grocery chain in Arizona at the time. They officially went out of business in 1987. This would be a very pivotal time in my life for which I would discover years later on New Year's Eve of 1995, a day I'll never forget.

The day I accidentally met Steven Spielberg's mother, Leah "LeeLee" Adler, after having a difficult time with my brother Mel, who was working for me at the time. As we were on our way to the airport, my brother reached over and turned off the engine then threw the keys out of the van, yelling at me, then smiling saying this, "Now how are you going to get to the airport on time?" I was so mad at him, really why, why, after I had the van fixed that he and his wife left broken down in Arizona, just sitting in our mom's carport.

I used my credit card to fix it. It cost me over twelve hundred dollars to do it luckily my sister in-law found the keys within two minutes. I later found out that he was jealous that my life was starting to take shape with a promising career on the horizon. After everything my brother and I had been through together, I never expected this. However, it's like my mentor, the Late Great Adam Roarke, once said, "Anthony, you have to find the positive in the negative." Adam died on April 27th, 1996, and I still miss him to this day.

It was because of that seed he planted in my mind that I didn't reach over and hit my brother in the face. Every single second and minute that passed, I heard Adam's voice in my head indirectly with those very words, "find the positive in the negative," saying directly to me to pay close attention, something good was going to come from this, and it did. Even though I didn't get to go to the New Year's Eve party in the Hollywood Hills where a lot of the known producers and directors were going to be on New Year's Eve. I was invited by my friend and acting teacher, Betty Saint George. I no longer had the address to get there due to the fact I left my itinerary in the console in the van and didn't realize it at the time because of all the excitement with my brother. I did meet Stephen Spielberg's mother, though, at her restaurant, the *Milky Way* on Pico Blvd. I accidentally found it on New Year's Eve.

Funny thing though, I didn't even know who she was until I went to use the restroom and upon returning to my table. There were at least a dozen or so Stephen Spielberg movie posters on the walls. As I walked by the poster with Tom Hanks' face on it, the movie was *BIG*. It was then that I realized Anne Spielberg was in the credits as a producer. She's Stephen Spielberg's younger sister. It was then that I realized that Leah Adler was

Stephen Spielberg's mother. I also learned that she and Mrs. Bayless were very good friends, small world, isn't it?

Even though we became friends, it was short-lived as I would eventually have to return to Avondale, Arizona, as my mother's health was declining, and none of my siblings were stepping up to the plate. So, I had decided to do it after much thought and careful consideration. I would officially be leaving L.A. In 2001, I officially left.

In mid-November of 1996, I called my agent Don Gerler and told him I was considering going home for Thanksgiving and Christmas in case he needed to contact me for an audition that might have been coming up. We talked for about four minutes, he agreed that going home for the holidays would probably be a good idea, as the entertainment industry was slowing down due to the holiday hiatus. Well, he was partly right on that note.

So, I decided to go back to Phoenix and spend some quality time with my mother, family, and friends. I even made some new friends. The day after Thanksgiving when I was hired to work on a Christmas tree lot, I believe the name of the company was *Great Northern Christmas Trees*. This actually would be a major blessing in my future, I just didn't know it yet. It was a win-win situation as I made some very good money up until Christmas Eve. Unfortunately, everything has its price. A week before Christmas, my agent called me on my PageNet pager service, "Anthony, it's Don Gerler, call me ASAP." My heart skipped a beat. I knew it was good news until he found out I wasn't in L.A. Apparently, he'd forgotten about our former discussion before I left for the holiday season.

He proceeded to give me all the information and even asked if he could fax me the sides. And then it happened as soon as I gave him an Arizona fax number for Kinko's, he got dead quiet, then calmly said, "You're in Arizona, what the hell are you doing in Arizona kid?" I told him you told me to go; he must have forgotten he said that.

I told him just send me the sides, "I can be back in L.A. by 7:30 a.m."

He said, "No, can't do that, sorry kid it wasn't meant to be. There'll be other opportunities though. Happy Holidays and thanks for getting back to me so quickly." My heart sunk when I found out it was for a lead in a remake of a former Television series wow.

I would return to L.A. in mid-January of 1997. Upon my return, my then-former *Playboy* playmate girlfriend at the time had decided to kick me out because of certain things she wanted me to do with her sexually that I refused to do based on my beliefs. As well as the fact she was also a psychic, apparently she was sensing I was beginning to lose interest in continuing our relationship.

It was obvious she wasn't happy about that; it was obvious she wanted revenge because she knew I was going to be leaving her in the near future. When I returned to L.A., after the holidays she gave me the boot, told me I needed to move out as her mother was going to be living with her for a while, ouch. Hell hath no fury like a woman scorned. Don't get me wrong she was beautiful in every sense of the word. The only problem was she was a bit too controlling. I wasn't about to go through that again after ten years with my ex-wife Tamara, no way Jose, was that going to happen again.

My goals and interests had changed; I was focusing on my then acting career as a future leading man in the entertainment industry. For two more years, I would do nothing but auditions and take acting classes and workshops with well-known casting directors until 1999. I would land a supporting role as Frederick Nietzsche in a movie titled *Existential Surfers*.

By the middle of 1999, I would unexpectedly be heading back to Arizona as my mom got really sick. The neighbors didn't even know what was wrong with her; said it was probably just a really bad cold, it wasn't, she had walking pneumonia. I knew that when I saw her because I had walking pneumonia before. It was more than obvious, I was going to be moving back to Arizona real soon.

My mother, according to the doctor in the ER, said that she wouldn't have made it through the night if I hadn't been there to bring her in, as the fluids had already been in her lungs for quite some time. The doctor told me, "You saved your mother's life; she's lucky you showed up when you did. You're more than her son; you're her Guardian Angel." It must have been fate that led me back to Arizona just in the nick of time as my mother was barely able to breathe.

These incidents, these trials and tribulations, were preparing me for what I was to do and become. People today need to pay attention because our trials and tribulations are training grounds, learning mechanisms to teach us. They're actually part of the very essence that will define who and what we become. What do you want to become when you grow up is the question, do you know?

In September of 1999, I was living with my mother and working at *Food City* as a grocery night stocker. They later gave me keys, which I didn't want. It was a setup, and I knew it, as they had bought *Southwest Supermarkets*. They just didn't want me to know it, as *Southwest Supermarkets* had unjustifiably terminated my employment in the early part of 1996, right before I moved to L.A., Los Angeles, California, to pursue my acting career.

It took me exactly four months to get a reputable SAG agent. I was immediately signed on with The Don Gerler Agency. I didn't know it at the time, but it turned out that Don Gerler and Adam Roarke were related, they were brothers. I never knew Adam had a brother named Don Gerler until Don himself told me. And he was a reputable agent as well.

After I signed on with him and his partner Danny, I asked Don one last question before I left his office that day, "So you're Adam Roarke's brother, why didn't Adam tell me he had a brother who was a Hollywood

Agent when I was studying and learning under him in Las Colinas, Texas?"

Don said, "If he had told you then, do you think you still would have moved to L.A.? Would it have been enough of a challenge for you to pursue your dream of becoming a leading man?"

I paused for a brief moment looking directly at him and said, "Probably not, I see your point."

Then he asked me about TJ. "This TJ Myers, what can you tell me about her? Does she have a great attitude? Is she easy to work with? What kind of actress is she?"

I didn't say a word for almost three seconds, I knew he wanted an answer. I paused for about three seconds due to the fact that TJ and I had a bit of a, let's just say it was a big misunderstanding at the time. I then replied, "She's alright, she's a professional, knows her craft, takes direction well, yeah she's good. Why do you ask?"

"I'm thinking about signing her, you just made my decision a lot easier, thank you, Anthony."

"You're welcome, Don," then I turned and left. I was pumped up, the excitement was running through my veins. For I had officially achieved the impossible. I had signed with a very well-known Hollywood Agent. Nothing's gonna stop me now. Even though I was close to living in my truck at the time, which did happen by the way when I returned to L.A. after the holidays except this time I had a few grand in my pocket.

This time things were different. I could feel it, I sensed it even though I missed an opportunity to be cast in *The Young and The Restless*, thanks to my former relationship counselor/entertainment manager. I knew it wasn't over. I was still paying my dues though! Nothing in this world that's worth fighting for ever comes easy. It all comes down to this haunting saying, to this day I can still hear her words (Bobby Ball) my former and very first talent agent in Phoenix, Arizona saying these very words. "HOW BAD DO YOU WANT IT."

We're all here for a reason, it's through our trails and tribulations that we'll discover our reason for being. For what doesn't break us, can make us. Just like gold, as it goes through the purification process to make it pure .99999, one hundred percent gold. We must also go through a process. And through that process, we are able to effectively change the world into a better place. For even a child before being born came from two seeds coming together. If faith is like a mustard seed, which spreads quickly, and it only starts with one seed. Then why can't we do the same?

Through my own trials and tribulations, this is what I learned from my experiences. And the words of a very wise soul (Adam Roarke), find the positive in the negative. Are you starting to get the picture? It would be one year later in October of 1999, that *Food City* (Bashes) fired me. Danny Garcia my then store manager first suspended me for some major BS. He later told his bosses that I quit.

That was a complete lie he made up to save his own butt and stopped me from getting unemployment checks. Companies often will lie about this to avoid paying out this unemployment benefit. I had turned in multiple health violations that I informed the health department about. That were never addressed due to the nature of Danny's carefree attitude.

Instead of being grateful that I brought these things to his attention. He became combative with me when I pointed out these health issues. "Really, you're a store manager and you don't care, are you serious?" I told him I remember the days where you could pretty much literally eat off the floor of the store, all store's floors actually. In the early to late '80s, you could eat off the floor if you wanted to. That's how clean they were. "What the hell happened?"

He just said "Times are different now, people just don't care anymore."

I looked at him and said this! "What, do my ears deceive me? Did you just say people don't care anymore?"

He then said, "Go home and forget about this place for the next couple of days. We may not like it, but that's just how it is now, our ways aren't theirs. This younger generation isn't just disrespectful of authority, it's lazy, undisciplined, doesn't give a damn about us or our work ethics. It's a losing battle human resources, the law, seems to protect them from real bullshit. Bullshit, they perpetuated and continued to practice. You're not going to change that. So do us both a favor right now and go home. Think about what I said, and start fresh, ok."

I didn't say a word, I shook my head and walked over to the time clock and punched out. When I left the store I felt like I'd been transported to another dimension in time. Somewhere in a distant galaxy far, far away plotting and planning my way on how to get back home.

Back home, to where common sense was still valued, where people were never easily offended. They laughed, joked, and shared stories- great stories, actually. Where they had competitive spirits, not in an egotistical way, but a healthy way. And the biggest one of them all the icing on the cake. We always would shut the bullies down. In their world it was completely the opposite, now the one bullying people was looked at as a victim. "What the hell happened?" How could this have happened? I'll tell you what happened for some unknown reason we said goodbye to common sense. And let the Government decide for us. We then had police knocking on our doors for unknown reasons. Like this one! "The reason we're here is because a concerned neighbor called us, we just wanted to be sure every-thing's okay."

Then I'd ask them who called. "We can't volunteer that kind of information sir, it's a violation of privacy."

"What, are you kidding?"

"No, I'm not kidding."

I looked him right in his eyes and said, "Doesn't the United States Constitution state that I have a right to confront my accusers?"

He paused for a brief second, then said, "You're correct, sir, however, that's in a court of law only, of which you are granted that privilege."

Then I said, "Granted that privilege, are you serious? And just how am I going to be able to file a court petition without a name?" I then added, "Then why doesn't it say those exact words 'granted privilege' in the Constitution?"

He then said, "I don't know."

"You don't know, yet you're a police officer," I replied, "Wow, something really messed up here."

Now, don't get me wrong here, I don't hate cops, and I respect authority as long as it's a fair and just authority. Unfortunately, it doesn't appear to be so anymore. Now is the time for all God-loving, fearing men to come together for the greater good. Our United States currency is next to worthless now. Was that planned? Very possible it was. They're trying to herd us around like cattle, cattle that pays their outrageous salaries.

America, she's going through some major BS right now. Her trials and tribulations have exceeded her ability to bounce back. She's no longer physically, economically, emotionally, spiritually, or financially strong due to the fact that practically every single government representative appears to be on the take. If they're not on the take, then they need to do the job We The People expect them to do. After all, isn't that why we agreed to pay taxes in the first place? According to the US Constitution, it is!

Americans used to be physically strong, ambitious, lean mean fighting machines, responsible people who took care of their own. If charity begins at home, then why are our tax dollars paying for everything and everyone else but not the interests of the American people? There's an old saying I heard a lot growing up: 'Sweep your own doorstep before you sweep someone else's.' It's simple to figure out the true meaning here: take care of your own business first before you decide to help others. Apparently, it appears our government officials have either forgotten this, or they never cared to begin with.

If the American people don't start to hold all of its political leaders responsible for this crap, it's not going to end well for the American Taxpayers or America. Now is the time for all God-loving, fearing, brave men to come to the aid of each and every American Taxpayer. We, The People of the United States of America, must legally put our foot on the neck of the snake that's robbing us all blind and stop the insanity now, once and for all.

It's our moral and civil duty to make sure our politically appointed leaders that we voted for in the first place keep their morals and conscience to serve and protect the interests of America and the American Taxpayers, aka their bosses. If they fail to do so, contact the attorney general's office night and day. Record live feeds of us doing this and put it on social media platforms, share the messages with one another until they can no longer take the political heat.

Then, after they've continuously refused to make things right, use the United States of America's Constitution against them. From there, take our case to the Supreme Court and demand that each and every one of them be charged with treason against America and We The People, aka American Taxpayers. Then watch how quickly the tides will change.

Einstein said it best when asked the question: "Are you afraid of evil men?"His response was something like this: "I am not afraid of evil men, I'm afraid of the good men who do nothing to stop them. For when good men do nothing, evil triumphs.' That's what I'm afraid of."

In other words, man up. It's time to clean house. We can no longer turn away from what's happening to our country. I told some of my coworkers in the warehouse I worked in that 'The United States of America' is dangerously close to becoming the next third world country just like Venezuela did in 2019.

If we don't start holding our Government one hundred percent accountable and demand that our borders are secured and stop this BS about thousands of illegal immigrants coming here illegally that skipped five to six countries just to claim political asylum here in America, which is illegal as hell and considered a treasonous act, punishable by law with a trial being held by a United States Military Tribunal with severe legal consequences, possibly a death sentence.

We The People must hold all those responsible for their cold, self-serving, calculated, selfish, prideful actions that are destroying our country.

After all, We The People are their real bosses. We not only have an obligation to ourselves, we have an obligation to the world. If The United States of America falls, the world economy falls. We can't allow this to happen. Now is the time for all good and moral men to come to the aid of their country.

Chapter 4

Unseen Acts of Kindness

The Unsung Heroes Among Us: Stories of Anonymous Good Deeds

I have always strived to be anonymous when doing good deeds and serving my fellow mankind. It's just a natural thing that has always been a big part of who I am. It's in my DNA. My father was an unsung hero just as I am today. However, since my dad is no longer among us, I feel it is only fitting to tell his story.

This will be based on what he shared with me, and maybe even some of my siblings, or maybe not. Maybe he just wanted me to know this because he noticed something different in me from my brothers and sisters. After all, none of them walked from Avondale to Glendale or Phoenix with him. I was the only one who he ever did that with, and since it would take us hours to get from point A to point B, we talked a lot about many different subjects - the wars that he served in, how he had just turned 18 and received a letter from Uncle Sam that went something like this: "Greetings, you have been selected to serve God and Country."

Really, on your eighteenth birthday, that's one hell of a kick in the ass - to be taken right out of school on your eighteenth birthday just to go home and tell your mother you love her and kiss her goodbye, all in five minutes. Then you catch a train heading to your brand new home with your new Momma, Papa, and big brother, not even knowing what to expect once you arrive for basic training preparation.

An eighteen-year-old boy, who was no longer a boy, unexpectedly became a man at that very moment. An eighteen-year-old boy who, after two years of serving in World War II, would become a Sargent in the US Army. Who trained other newly drafted eighteen-year-olds on how to survive on the front line. Yep, that's where my dad was put right smack dab in the middle of it all. At first, the young draftees gave him some lip after ordering them to dig their own foxholes. They laughed and said, "We ain't digging no damn foxholes."

My dad didn't blink. Instead, he looked them straight in the eyes, tossed the shovel aside, and said, "Suit yourselves."

As my dad was walking away, they were laughing and making fun of him. All of a sudden, they started to hear whistles. Those weren't just whistles; they were bullets flying by them. You see, when bullets pass by you, they sound like whistles. My dad knew that from that point on, he'd have no more problems with any of them ever refusing to dig a foxhole ever again. He actually sent a couple of men out to get the scared ladies. As they pulled them back to my dad's location, a nice big foxhole, he looked them all in the eyes, walking back and forth in front of them.

Very quietly, like a lion getting ready to pounce and working very hard not to laugh, he just said this, "Next time, follow my orders. You just might continue living, breathing, and walking on this earth. Is that clear?"

A big, "Yes, sir" was heard from all three soldiers. The corporal gave them a bit of a lecture after my dad was through talking to them, which apparently changed their minds about my dad. You see, my dad had been on that front line for two years.

He never even got so much as a scratch. He never been shot in those two years from what I can remember based off of what he told me, except for the bullet that hit his Heart Shield Bible, which made him fly backward on his butt, with a bit of blood running down his uniform. He believed he might have been dying. Until the medic came around and removed the now bullet-imprinted Bible in my dad's front pocket. He believed that because he had played it forward, expecting nothing in return from those he helped, he'd been given a second chance at life. In other words, he was not only blessed, he was grateful.

The information I'm about to share with all of you now was once highly classified (unbelievable) but highly classified. If the truth had gotten out to the civilian world then, let's just say the riots, aka insurrections, after George Floyd died would never have happened. What my father said is true. It's also very disheartening that someone from higher up in the ranks would do such a thing to any human being, regardless of someone's race, creed, or color.

In 1944, our Black American brothers or African American brothers, were put on the war front lines with a 38 snub-nosed revolver to fight for God and Country. A 38 snub-nosed has a very limited range in distance -

they can only fire fifteen to twenty-five yards away, that's roughly around 75 to 80 feet. What do you think the odds of you surviving are going to be on a heavy military artillery-filled War Front line using a 38 snub-nose, 50/50 not even, more like 10% if you're lucky. Now, I told you pretty much from the very beginning of the story, basically my dad grew up learning from the school of hard knocks. An interesting thing about members of that school is they recognize their own.

My father was about to change two of their lives forever, and he would pay a very high price for doing it. He didn't care. Right is right, and wrong is wrong, and this was so very, very, wrong. My dad couldn't take it as he watched two African American brothers being pinned down by heavy fire. They could hear the bullets whistling over their heads. They had been brought into this God-forsaken War with one guarantee - they were meant to die. But fate stepped in and changed their destinies for the rest of their lives.

How, you ask? Well, it's kind of a Russian roulette thing, if you will. Remember when I told you my father was the sergeant after two years of serving on the front lines? That gave him access to weapons. At that point in time, a highly advanced weapon known as the M1 Garand had a firing range of up to 500 yards. Are you beginning to get the picture? My father decided, after his commanding officer gave him a direct order to not help the two African American brothers out and let nature just take its course, yeah right. Can you call bullshit?

This was in no way, shape, or form natural in any way. They were screaming for help, which my father answered. He threw two M1 Garands within their reach. I think their response was this, "Much obliged, Sarg, thank you." After things calmed down and the firing ceased, his commanding officer, my father's commanding officer, wanted to have a word with my father.

He told him, "I gave you a direct order not to do it." And the two African Americans were standing beside him, and he said, "This isn't over," and walked away. "I'll deal with you later, Sergeant."

The next day, early in the morning, my father was called to his CO's (commanding officer's) office. He proceeded to reprimand my dad for the heroic act of saving the two African Americans on the front line. He gave him seven and a half weeks of KP (kitchen patrol), aka "kitchen police." He ordered him to clean a five-thousand-square-foot warehouse with a toothbrush until it was clean to his liking. Then he gave him seven and a half weeks of

KP peeling potatoes, too. So, it is what it is - kitchen patrol or kitchen police still sucks, right?

The point is simple. My father was willing to give something up for the greater good, even if it meant him losing his life. Most people today would probably laugh at this heroic act because they lack one very important thing. That one thing is called common sense. Unfortunately, most people don't seem to have or care about it in today's society.

Well, I have some sobering news for you. That's right, I said sobering, because this world today is either drunk, high, or blind. Most people today only seem to care about getting high, sex, and money. They don't see the bigger picture simply because they don't want to. For them, it's normal to laugh at someone who falls down on the sidewalk as they ready their phones to shoot video of what just happened. They are amused by watching another human being suffer. They'd rather laugh at them than help them.

I'll give you an example. I was visiting a friend in Los Angeles, California back in 2004. I believe it was around April! As I was leaving the parking lot of a *RiteAid* drug store in North Hollywood located off of Magnolia Blvd, I noticed two young men walking towards me asking me for help. As they got closer, I noticed something very strange and odd. Something was very off as the younger one appeared to be experiencing vertigo; he continued to go in and out.

I then took his pulse to check his heartbeat, and it was really slow. The other guy looked at me and asked if I was a doctor. I said no, then asked him, "What did you give him?"

He more or less panicked and started laughing nervously, and then spoke. "It's not drugs, it's only alcohol," he said.

I replied, "Only alcohol?"

He responded, "Yeah, that's all, it's just alcohol."

Then he darted away, leaving me with the sick and weak kid. I walked with him, keeping my left arm around his left shoulder. I told him, "You need to go to the hospital."

He replied, "No, no, hospital, my parents would kill me."

I said, "I doubt that. Maybe they'll make you wish you were dead, but they're not going to kill you." He still refused to go to the hospital. Luckily, I had grown up around a few alcoholics.

I remembered what my mom and dad had done when my brother got alcohol poisoning. They kept him warm, walking, talking, rehydrated him, and laid him on his side to prevent choking if he vomited. I did everything my parents did, and after six or seven hours, he began to show signs of recovery. He thanked me for staying with him. I tried to get him to press charges on the so-called 25-year-old friend who bought him the alcohol, but he refused.

The sad thing about this encounter was that the people who witnessed him barely being able to walk just kept laughing at him. Especially the ones at Venice Beach who kept saying mean things like, "You two sure make a cute couple," "What did you give him? Were you trying to get lucky?" That did it for me. I confronted the punk who said this. I wanted to hit him, but I didn't.

I looked him straight in the eye and said, "If this is what the world is going to be like, I am so glad that I came from a generation that respects and cares about life. Do you actually find this funny, you sick fuck?"

He turned and walked away. As I was turning the corner, a police officer approached us. She said, "You need to get your son out of here, or we'd be riding downtown."

I smiled and said, "Thank you, officer, I will do that." The point here is simple: honor, integrity, respect, love, compassion – they need to return. There was only one being who ever lived on the planet who said, "Teach only love." They fall under that category, don't they?

Isn't it time for us to wake up, put on our big boy and big girl pants, change the status quo, take charge of the wheel, turn it in the right direction to ensure our future and the future of generations after us? Hopefully, they, in turn, will do the same for the generations to come, simply by teaching only love.

I'll leave you with another example of showing kindness and respect for those who are disabled. I was working for the *Harding Paint Company* in California, around L.A. County, painting houses. We painted celebrities' houses, lawyers' houses, even the house that was once owned by Thomas Dolby, the artist that wrote and produced the song "She Blinded Me with Science" or "Poetry in Motion." I also painted Tom Morello's house; he's the bass guitarist for *Rage Against the Machine*.

Yeah, I met a lot of very well-known people that I treated just like I would treat any other human beings – with respect, honor, and dignity. Speaking of dignity, I believe it was either May or June when I witnessed a bunch of gang members in a car harassing a young blind woman. They kept driving by her, trying to pull up her dress. I didn't wait a second and very slowly and quietly approached their vehicle. I was wearing dark sunglasses, had long hair (which I later cut), and was wearing a very long black leather coat tied tightly around my waist.

One of the gang members told me to mind my own business as he spat towards my feet. I smiled with a very sinister look, like Clint Eastwood as Dirty Harry or in any of his movies, even the spaghetti Westerns. Anyway, I adapted what he used, and I made it my own. As I went to grab the young blind woman's hand, she quickly, out of fear, pulled away. I got closer to her and whispered in her right ear, "I mean you no harm. Trust me, God told me to help you."

At that time, one of the gang members started to open the door. I quickly kicked it closed. They were officially pissed off at this point. The driver of the car noticed how calm I was remaining, which led him to believe that I might have a gun under my coat. At that point, the blind woman took my hand, and we quickly cut through a park. Luckily, she was familiar with it, and it turned out her apartment was about a block away.

Long story short, I escorted her to her apartment door, made sure she was safely inside. Before I left, she thanked me and asked who I was. I said, "I'm just someone who happened to be where God apparently needed me." As she put the key in her lock to open the door, she was apprehensive about going in and still apparently didn't trust me. I said, "It's okay, go on in, you're going to be alright." From that moment on, she knew it was no accident that I happened to be walking through the area that day. It was divine intervention that led me to her.

It was God who put me there at the right time and the right place when someone who couldn't defend herself needed a true warrior to even the score and get her safely home, which I did. I had witnessed too much violence growing up and seen too many abusive men beating on women as a young boy and young man. Enough was enough, and I had the skills and know-how to make a difference. If I could help them, I was going to do exactly that, simply because it was the right thing to do.

Now, let's fast forward to Phoenix, Arizona. It was around April of 1999. I still had my vision of becoming a leading man in California and still had my agent in Hollywood. I still had one foot in that door and another in the Phoenix, Arizona door. I was torn between two different places. My mother was starting to show beginning signs of Alzheimer's and dementia. They were subtle signs, but they were signs that something was wrong. I didn't realize at that time what exactly was going on with her.

I could sense that something wasn't right, so I stayed a little bit longer, about nine months longer. I ran back into Ken Byrum again when I stopped at one of the Food City stores on Buckeye Road in Phoenix to buy some deodorant, toothpaste, and soft drinks on the way home from my best friend's apartment who lived on Baseline Road with his former wife. It had been six years since I last saw Ken. He immediately recognized me, came over, and asked how life had been treating me.

Then he asked me where I had been. I said, "Hey Ken, I've been in L.A. pursuing other interests."

He said, "Are you going back anytime soon?"

I looked directly at him and said, "Probably not." He asked me if I was going to need a job. I said, "Maybe."

He said, "Go see Al. You remember Al, from Lucky's, Gemco. He's looking for night crew stockers. He's the manager of *Food City* off of 43rd Avenue and

McDowell Road. He'll hire you; he knows what you can do. Plus, he's hurting for good people with real grocery experience. He can't get anybody."

I thanked Ken for the information and said I might just do that. I went home, cooked my mother's dinner, set up a TV tray, and watched her favorite TV show, *The Nanny*. After attending to all of my mother's needs, I fell asleep, woke up around 9:00 AM, got cleaned up, took a shower and shaved. Then I jumped in the Toyota van that my brother Mel and his wife gave to my mother.

I drove over to *Food City*, met with Al, who immediately recognized me. We talked for about three minutes, then walked up the stairs to his office where I filled out an employment application. Three days later, after my UA came back negative, he called me up and asked when I could start. I said, "Tomorrow."

He replied, "Great, congratulations, and welcome back to the industry." I said thanks, hung up the phone, and my heart sank as I noticed my dream was starting to slip away.

My excitement of becoming a leading man was still there deep down inside of me. My heart was still longing to be back in L.A. working in TV and film as an actor. My mentor's voice (Adam Roarkes) was still in my head, talking to me and telling me that I would accomplish and achieve my goal, my dream of becoming a leading man in some way, somehow, somewhere would have to be put on temporary hold.

I felt lost and confused, moving back to the hell hole I grew up in, where I had been disrespected, abused, and treated like crap. I kept thinking, "Why can't I catch a break? Why can't my brothers, sister, and family give me the emotional and moral support I need to help me obtain my dreams? Why couldn't they help out with our mother instead of just leaving me with all the responsibility of taking care of her?"

I started to feel like I was the prodigal son. Apparently, the only thing my family ever seemed to really approve of me doing was working in the grocery business. I was always praised by my family members and relatives for advancing so quickly in that industry, versus the entertainment industry. Why couldn't they see that the industry was draining the very life out of me? My heart and soul were crying for me to find a way out. Apparently, God had other plans for my future.

For I was not only the prodigal son. Years later, I would eventually become the unsung hero just like my father, but under different circumstances. Nobody, until now, would know what I gave up to help my aging mother. Only a handful of my closest friends knew the truth. My so-called neighbors just assumed I couldn't make it in the entertainment industry. They believed, because their lives were empty and somewhat mundane, that it is what it is. They thought I was probably just making everything up about having an agent and meeting quite a few very well-known actors, producers, and directors in L.A. and Arizona.

They believed I only came back because I couldn't make it in the entertainment industry. Nothing but lies. Even though before I officially moved back to Arizona, I had asked them to help me get help for my mother . Their response was this: It's not our place to get involved in your business, even after they had claimed from years prior that we were family to them. By the way, did I mention that they were black or, if you prefer, African American?

That was the summer of 1999. It was also the first time since 1992 that I'd seen my oldest brother Mark, who got in some pretty hot water with the Richardson, Texas police department, that could have gotten him locked up for many, many years. Because of my abilities of always finding a way to turn the tables around in practically every situation I've ever encountered in my life, when my mother called me, I could sense before she even said it that my oldest brother Mark was in trouble. She then asked me over the phone if I knew an attorney who could help my brother. I did; his name was Tom Clayton. He was a former prosecutor for the City of Dallas, Texas. He was also my personal business lawyer and friend. I had introduced him to Tom Clayton at a local event in Duncanville, Texas, of which Tom was a guest.

Immediately after introducing my brother to him, Tom whispered in my left ear (my brother was standing on my right side), and he said, "Is he innocent?"

I said, "I think so."

He said, "What do you mean you think so?" I then proceeded to explain that my brother had an alcohol addiction and said he couldn't remember because he blacked out.

Then he asked me again, "Do you believe he's innocent?" I said yes. Tom then, without hesitation, went over and asked my brother a few more questions.

He gave my brother a very generous offer to represent him for a very modest fee of two hundred dollars. Mark reached out to shake his hand in agreement. Tom then said, "It's only because you're his brother that I'm going to do this for two hundred dollars, you do understand that." My brother didn't say a word, he just shook his head in agreement. Tom then proceeded with the following. "There are three conditions that go with this deal. One, you listen to everything I tell you to do. Two, you do exactly what I tell you to do when I tell you to do it. And Three, you're going to turn yourself in when I instruct you to do so."

It was at that point my brother said, "Wait, you want me to turn myself in?"

Tom said, "Yeah, do you have a problem with that?" Tom then excused himself for a moment, pulled me away from my brother, then said, "he's going to panic, if he panics and runs like a rabbit. I can't help him. Tell him if he plays ball with me. I believe I can get the judge to reduce it to ten years deferred adjudication. Now, that's the best-case scenario, and I believe it's obtainable. It all depends on who the Judge is going to be."

Tom shook my hand, went to shake my brother's hand, my brother didn't reciprocate. Tom then pointed at me and said, "Don't forget what I said."

I immediately went up to my brother and said, "What the hell was that? Tom Clayton is one of the best

Lawyers in all of Dallas, he's also my friend. He knows the law and what he's talking about, and you just snubbed him like he's a piece of crap."

At that point, my brother said, "I don't even know this guy, or any of your friends. Hell, I don't even know if this guy can even get me off."

At that point, I went over to my brother, looked him straight in the eyes. And said, "Tom Clayton has never lost a case. You're not going to find another lawyer in all of Dallas, Texas with that kind of track record who will take your entire case for two hundred dollars. Let him help you, trust me with Tom representing you, there's a ninety-nine point nine percent chance you'll walk right out of that courtroom a free man."

Later that night, my brother made a long-distance phone call from a payphone at the convenience store about a block away from the luxury apartment complex I was living at in the early nineties. It was a collect call to our mother. At the time, I was just getting out of the shower when my phone rang, it was my mother. She asked me if Tom Clayton was truly interested in helping my brother. I said, "Yes, but he has to do exactly what Tom has instructed him to do."

She then suggested we both come home for Thanksgiving. I said, "Actually, that's a good idea. I can take him to see Mario. With Mario's legal knowledge, that just might swing him back in Tom's direction. Ok, I'll ask him, we can leave tonight, love you, mom."

At that point, my brother just walked in the door. It was about 8:oo PM. He said, "Was that Mom?"

I said, "Yes, and we're going to Phoenix tonight." At first, my brother was hesitant due to the current situation then finally agreed.

Fifteen hours later, we arrived in Arizona just in time for Thanksgiving dinner. The day after Thanksgiving, I took him to see my best friend Mario Grana, who apparently after hearing all the details of the whole legal mess, agreed with Tom Clayton. Mario also said that to retain a lawyer for two hundred dollars is unheard of, their fee is normally like four to six thousand just to retain them. That doesn't include filing fees, paperwork fees, logged attorney hours.

Mario then looked at my brother and said, "I've known Jerry since nineteen eighty-seven. If he says this Tom Clayton knows how to get your ass out of the legal hot water you're in right now, with deferred adjudication, and he's a former prosecutor, for two hundred dollars then guarantees you a ninety-nine point nine percent chance of walking out of that courtroom without any cuffs or ankle bracelet. I'd say take the deal, go back to Dallas as soon as possible, and hire that man."

After spending about an hour or two at Mario's house enjoying a family backyard barbeque of steak and smoked Italian sausage, Mark and I eventually left the party and drove back to our hometown, Avondale. Mom had just finished cooking us up some leftover turkey and stuffing with a baked potato loaded with butter, sour cream, and chives. Even though we'd just eaten at Mario's, we still sat at the table and ate with our mother. She said grace, blessing our food, then asked me, "So what did Mario say?"

I said, "He basically agreed with Tom Clayton, told Mark to take the deal. No lawyer, that he knows of would ever make that kind of offer, especially a former prosecuting attorney."Mom then asked my brother what do you want to do.

He got up, walked in the living room dead quiet, mumbled the words, "Deferred adjudication doesn't mean it goes away," then threw his hands frantically into the air. "I don't know, I don't know who to trust, what to do, I don't know what you're both telling me, or asking me to do." Then it happened, my brother broke down in tears. I've never really seen my brother cry before.

Mom and I went to comfort him, but he retreated to our old bedroom, crying his butt off. My brother's spirit had been broken. From that point on, he would never have been the same. My mother walked calmly down the hallway. She knocked on the door, asking him if she could come in and talk to him. My brother didn't answer. Mom tried to open the door, it was locked. Eventually, my brother opened the door and let her in, then quickly closed the door, apparently he didn't want me in the room for some reason.

Three days later, we returned to Dallas, Texas. My brother's wife, Leslie, had just sent him a message on his paging service while we were still on the road. The message said good news, call me right away love Leslie. When we arrived I would find out that my brother had been holding back some valuable information about a twelve thousand dollar insurance settlement from an accident that wasn't his fault. At first, I was a little pissed, then I calmed down and said, "Your life's about to change, you're being blessed, don't screw it up."

"Call Tom Clayton, hire him for the two hundred dollars. Then turn yourself in when he tells you to. He'll bail you out, you'll get to spend Christmas with your family. Within a year or two this will all be over." He then said this as he got out of my truck, "thanks, I'll think about it." Apparently, Leslie needed Mark to go to the Lawyer's office to sign the check or document to hand them a twelve thousand dollar insurance settlement check , payable to them only. Leslie was parked at the convenience store down the street from my apartment.

Even though my brother kept this information under his belt, I felt a sigh of relief at that moment. Then why was it that I had this gut feeling that my brother was about to make some very bad financial moves that would not only affect my mother's life in the future but would also affect mine.

Christmas was five days away when my brother decided to go shopping with his half of the insurance settlement. First, he bought Leslie a wedding ring which he never apparently gave her. Then, he bought toys for their children with the rest of it. He bought himself some clothes, took Leslie to the Hilton, got a room under her name, took her out for dinner and dancing at the finest restaurant in Dallas. Big mistake; all the money was gone.

I called him a fool, and he retaliated with, "I don't know what the future holds for me. This is the first time in my life I've ever had any real money. Apparently you've had real money before. I haven't. I don't know if I'm going to jail or even prison for that matter. This was the one time in my life I could make things right for my own family just in case I did end up in jail. At least I could do this one last thing for my family."

"If I were you, I would be calling Tom Clayton and beg him to represent me. Because now what are you going to do?"

He shook his head and said, "You can't even know what I'm going through right now. So how can you stand there and tell me what to do?" he continued.

I replied, "Apparently I can't, you're right. I don't know what you're going through or what you're feeling as you're going through all of this. But, if you want pity, you're not going to get it from me."

He turned around, jumped in his truck shaking his head in disbelief. Then, with his back turned to me, he said, "Fine, if you're not going to help me, I'll call Mom."

I warned him, "Leave our mother out of this. If I find out you got any money from her to hire a lawyer, I'll kick your ass."

Later that night, I got a call from my mom. She wasn't very happy to hear my voice. She actually said very little at first, and then she let me have it. "You said you would help your brother; he's scared and very confused right now. If you can't help him, I will." My intuition went into overdrive, and in just a few seconds, I saw flashes of the future in my mind's eye. I saw my mother's house being taken away from her, my mother giving Mark money for a lawyer, leaving her close to pretty much being homeless. Although that never happened, I made sure of that by returning to Arizona to take care of her in the early part of 2000, as it was more than obvious her cognitive abilities were slipping badly.

It was then that I found out about the second mortgage she got to help my brother get out of trouble. My mom had gotten a second mortgage back in 1992; she only needed six more payments for her house to be paid off, free and clear. My Aunt Frances and Uncle Buddy went with her to look over the paperwork before she signed it all. This is where everything started to quietly nosedive for the next ten years.

When my mom asked me to take a look at the mortgage agreement, I immediately spotted the tricky wording culprit, that wording was 'variable rate.' Now here's the part I don't understand – we come from a family of property and commercial real estate people. How could they not know what 'variable rate' means? Even I knew what it meant. It's a sneaky way of disguising its true meaning; the interest rate can be increased, which causes the monthly payments to rise.

I knew then that I had to move quickly, as my mom was now in danger of losing her house she could no longer afford; now with new monthly inflated interest payments thanks to my older brother who actually put her in this financial hot seat. I went into action right away. I called my best friend Mario, who had just gotten into real estate as a loan officer. The only way out at this point was to fix up the house and sell it for a much bigger profitable margin. For almost a month, I worked on that house night and day. I painted it inside and outside, laid tile throughout the entire house. I put in over ten thousand dollars' worth of unpaid labor, as this was a labor of love. I spent time and money which I didn't really have to help my mom out.

After I was done, she thanked me. The noisy neighbors couldn't believe their eyes as the house looked like it had been painted by a professional painter. It had been — me. I was the professional painter who learned to paint professionally when I worked for the Harding Paint

Company for about a year when I lived in L.A in the late nineties.

Now, the next step was to sign all the paperwork, put the real estate sign in the front yard, and sell the house. Then, take that money and buy her a brand new home, paid for free and clear. The plan was working; I found a bigger beautiful house for her, a manufactured home. The price was exactly thirty-five thousand dollars total out the door.This house was beautiful inside and out; it didn't even look like a manufactured home. I even found a three-quarter-acre lot to put her new home down on in a much quieter, respectable neighborhood. Everything was coming together beautifully until the noisy neighbors and my Aunt Frances got involved.

The new issue was the three-quarter-acre lot and the monthly payment of six hundred and eighty dollars, simply because they were blinded by the truth. What they chose to see was a lie that was unfortunately created in all their minds. I worked very hard to attempt to open their eyes to the truth - that it wasn't me who had gotten my mother in this financial money pit; it was my oldest brother's doing that created this mess, not mine.

The next thing I heard while at work was, "Your aunt and one of your mom's neighbors just pulled up the real estate sign that Joe put in the front yard. My boss isn't happy, call me when you get this message." The mortgage company was threatening to take my mother to court; fortunately, that didn't happen.

Thanks to my best friend Mario, who convinced his boss that my mom was going through the beginning stages of Alzheimer's and Dementia, as he had witnessed her lack of focus and train of thought getting progressively worse when visiting us and checking out the property to get an idea of what we're up against. No court case was ever filed from the mortgage company against her, and the mortgage company just washed their hands from the entire legally binding agreement. Thank you, Mario, for being there when my mom needed help.

Unfortunately, this situation had escalated to the point of no return. The neighbors had convinced my mom, due to her cognitive decline, to get a reverse mortgage – a very serious criminal act. It was a crime because my mother wasn't really aware of exactly what she was signing, or for that matter, what it really meant. The noisy neighbors failed to consult with me about any of this, and instead, they went down to the city court and helped my mom get an Order of Protection against me,

making all kinds of unbelievable written legal statements about me and my so-called estranged relationship
with my mother. In later years, they would deny they
wrote the now legally documented letters.

They never took responsibility for any of their actions;
instead, they kept pointing their finger at me, saying if I
hadn't deserted my mother, they would have never
stepped in. Deserted, really? What! I never deserted
her. You helped her legally and unethically remove me
from her place of residence.

They continued with this - you left her by your own
choosing, that's why we got involved. Are you kidding
me? Even though as a result of all of this, I became
homeless for over nine and a half months due to the
false accusations they made in the written documents,
aka legally binding letters. They never admitted any
wrongdoing on their part or even apologized.

There's an old saying: no good deed goes unpunished. Is
it true? In some situations, I'd say it is, not because you
did a good deed though. It's the lack of shared information that unknowingly punishes you. Why do you think
the Italians kept their friends close but their enemies
closer?

In today's society, most people I've encountered don't want to know or even hear the truth. They would much rather live in their own little safety-padded imaginary world, get high in the parking lots of their workplaces because they can't handle stress. Instead, they've become energy vampires, lying to cover their asses, receiving only a slap on the wrist because there appears to be no more accountability for one's actions.

Unless you're in your late forties and sixties, then you're held accountable because you know better. Even though the young punks, that's right I said young punks, never ever get reprimanded for their actions, causing a downward spiral in the quality of work in the workplace. This inadvertently causes a downward spiral with people not wanting to help anybody because they're afraid they're going to cause themselves a downward spiral.

This causes older caring people not wanting to help anybody anymore because they're afraid they're going to get in trouble for a bunch of prefabricated nonsense on the younger people's part. Yes, doing good deeds for those in need is still a very noble thing to do. Unfortunately, it is in serious danger of becoming extinct.

Chapter 5
Assembling the Team
By Forging Connections and Building Relationships. Using the Power of Unity in Making a Difference!

There is no "I" in team! I have always been a team player. However, in today's world, that's become almost obsolete, virtually non-existent. It seems that more and more people today just want to use you. We're no longer appreciated or respected for the skills we possess. Which is sad because there is actual power in uniting and working together. Why do you think they call America the United States of America? Think about it like this: if a house is divided, will it not fall? You better believe it will.

Abraham Lincoln knew it all too well when he was running for senator against Stephen Douglas in 1858. Lincoln coined the phrase "A house divided against itself cannot stand." Unfortunately, he didn't win a

Senate seat; he lost against Douglas. Two years later, Lincoln ran against him again, only this time it was for the race to the White House to become President. This time, the tables would turn in Lincoln's favor, making him the sixteenth President of the United States of America.

Was he talking about politicians or government in general? No, he was referring to bringing an end to slavery and uniting together to build a better, stronger country. The United States was not only the youngest country to end slavery, she was also one of the first to do so.

Today, in the twenty-first century, Americans seem to have forgotten and abandoned his warning. Most of us have become lazy, complacent couch potatoes, eating comfort foods, aka junk foods. No longer taking care of our bodies, not keeping ourselves physically fit or staying healthy anymore. Not even caring about anything or anyone, except going home, playing video games, and smoking vapor or pot.

They're getting high all the time, eating junk foods, becoming dangerously obese, getting on the computer and watching porn, or watching football on their sixty-inch big screen TV. Not a good equation. I mean, football's okay, but making it an obsession isn't. Obsessions are never healthy, period. Why do I care, you ask? Simple: if the younger generation doesn't get its shit together, there will be no more United States of America. It will be gone.

When we have tens of thousands of illegal immigrants crossing our borders every single day and skipping through six other countries just to claim political asylum in the good old U.S.A., and our government isn't doing a damn thing about it. That's not even an ethical act, it's also illegal, and that's a major slap in the face to the American taxpayers. Our so-called government isn't doing the job "We the People" paid them and continue to pay them to do.

Each and every one of them needs to be tried for treason in front of a military tribunal and sent to Guantanamo. Because of our government representatives' laid-back attitude, America is now experiencing a potentially hostile Trojan Horse takeover. What's even sadder is the fact that most of our youth can't even see it.

They get too easily overwhelmed by the little things in life, so they ignore the reality of everyday life by getting high all the time, even on the job, to escape reality just to feel good (comfortable) for a few hours. Can't they see they're setting themselves up for a potentially hostile takeover? In my time, we worked out, played sports like boxing, wrestling, weight lifting, baseball, football, track and field, shot put, archery, etc.

We set the bar high to challenge ourselves, to become better all the time. With anything that we undertook, good was never good enough. It was with our competitive nature that we conquered and triumphed. Just like our ancestors did when they were learning how to survive and thrive. Unfortunately, today that is not the case for America and her youth.

They've become too comfortable, while other countries like China and Russia are educating their youth to become scientists, doctors, lawyers, and positions such as these. Here in America, most of our youth are only interested in becoming movie stars, TV stars, public figures, digital creators, and money chasers. Now don't get me wrong here, I'm not saying these are bad professions to get into. What I'm saying is if everyone just keeps on deciding to be one of these, how will our country survive this downward trend? It won't.

I remember when I had my own business with my ex-wife back in the late eighties. We had a team, and it was because of our team that we became successful. In time, though, that ended due to the greed of other members of our team who were only thinking of themselves. This was the beginning of the selfish and self-serving generation that was beginning to show their ugly side with their greedy attitudes that eventually killed our business. She was also tired of getting dirty; refinishing antiques is a dirty business.

My ex eventually left me after that for a brief period of time. We later reunited and got back together when I agreed to move to Dallas, Texas, to be with her. Honestly, this wasn't part of my plan at the time. However, after my best friend told me it would be like six months before we could start our legal document prep company, I realized I didn't have six months to spare.

I was broke with no job and looking for work in a shitty economy. There weren't a whole lot of options there. It was either sink or swim. I chose to swim, so I got on a plane and started my new life in Dallas, Texas.

This would eventually open up another door of opportunity for me in the entertainment industry, working in and managing gentlemen's clubs in Dallas, Texas, after meeting Gary Dawn, a former professional NFL football player, who introduced me to Robert Bishop, who later introduced me to Randy Dumas. I found my new team. Or was I fooling myself and chasing shiny pennies

When I first arrived in Texas, I felt like I had been reborn. Everything was new to me as the only places I had ever known or been to until that point were Arizona and California. I had never flown anywhere until I met Tamara. She was different from all the other women I had dated - spunky, feisty, emotionally strong, and beautiful inside and out. It seemed that all she wanted from me was my love and support. However, she was also hiding something from me - she had been emotionally scorned by quite a few men from her past, which eventually hindered our relationship.

She was beautiful, but emotionally messed up - damaged goods. She also lied to me about moving to Dallas, Texas three weeks from the night we met. She said she was moving there to manage a well-known and popular five-star restaurant, and all she wanted to do was go out and have fun until she and her kids left for Texas. Yes, she was older than me, about fifteen years older, but she didn't look it - she looked great. I believed I had found my teammate, my confidant, my partner, my mate.

Ten years later, I would find out she wasn't exactly the woman I thought she was. Don't get me wrong here - I'm grateful for meeting her and the experience and time we had together. It became more and more evident she wasn't the team player I thought she was. She finally showed me, after ten years of an on-and-off relationship, just how selfish she could be, so I called it quits - or we called it quits, honestly, I think we both did.

Look, the point I'm making here isn't to point fingers or lay blame. That's not my intention at all. I'm simply pointing out that this was a losing situation from the start. If we had recognized it sooner, we probably wouldn't have even been together at all. We didn't really waste our time, though - being together, we learned a lot from one another, at least I did. Our relationship had come to a point of no return - it had been damaged to the point of no longer being salvageable.

She had gotten jealous of all the attention I was receiving and the things that I was doing, especially for the recognition I was receiving for my talents. I was officially entering the entertainment industry of acting and doing well. Tamara actually introduced me to it when she and her two daughters moved into my condo with me. I even had a shot at becoming the cover model on a romance novel, as well as a shot on a Soap.

She sabotaged it with the help of my business manager, Jackie. To this day, I could never figure out why my business manager wanted me to stay with Tamara. Do you see why having the right team is important now?

Others noticed her jealousy. She had no reason to be jealous - she was beautiful, a real head-turner. Did I mention that she was a former Playboy Bunny at the former downtown Phoenix Club at 3033 N. Central Avenue? We could have had a beautiful life together. Maybe I damaged it, or she damaged it, I don't really know.

Honestly, though, if the truth be known, we were both responsible for the damage that was done to our relationship. After going to counseling by myself, she didn't want to go with me at all. Even after I hinted it could help our relationship, she flat out refused, saying I was the one with the problem. Doesn't it take two to tango?

When we first met, it was magical. We worked together, played together, laughed together, shared our hopes and dreams with one another until we just didn't work anymore. I still loved her, though. Just no longer in love with her.

I mean she was a great person, a beautiful woman, fun, loving, vibrant, and exciting. She just didn't give me the same moral support I was giving her simply because she said it wasn't her thing to read movie scripts with me, among a few other things she was doing behind my back. She said she was sorry, but I should find someone or hire someone to read with me, so I did just that!

When Tamara was watching one of my scene study videotapes - yes, it was a VHS tape actually, after all, this is 1992 we're talking about here - she quickly noticed the blonde I was working with. She said very calmly and quietly, "Who's that?"

I said, "Oh, that's TJ, she's the actress I'm working with!"

Tamara very quietly and coyly responded with, "You're not going to be working with her anymore."

"Yes, I am. She's awesome and a great actress."

I knew too well that the green-eyed monster had just revealed itself, in more ways than one. Tamara knew then it would only be a matter of time before we both went our separate ways as we no longer worked together - our relationship had served its purpose. What I learned from it, in the end, was this: nothing would ever change for the better, it was time to move on. Although I am very grateful for the amount of time that we spent together.

Dallas, Texas had become a real burnout for me at this point. Before I officially left Texas, there were several profitable employment opportunities offered to me. I was presented with an opportunity to run a label printing company, "Label Sales," in Dallas, by my adopted stepdad, Jack Williams. His offer was very generous, by the way. Two months after that, I received another offer I was considering taking until my former club boss came back with a very lame offer after several attempts to negotiate a reasonable and fair offer, which he refused. I turned him down flat.

I reasoned with myself, if I couldn't love what I was doing for a living, then why do it? I knew exactly what I wanted to do, who I wanted on my team, and how I was going to get there once my journey started.

My journey, I wanted to be a movie star - nothing or nobody at that point was going to stop me from becoming a star. I was ready, I was focused, I mastered my craft thanks to Adam Roarke and The Film Actors Lab. I was ready to make my presence known to the world.

One thing I learned earlier in my life as a young boy who grew up overnight was this: it's God who decides what's best for us. Because when He's not included in our lives, things somehow eventually fall apart. You see what I learned is this: God is and always will be the Head Consultant to instruct us on what to do next. He puts the right people in our paths at the right time, sending us who to talk to and who to include on our team, which makes everything work. We then find the right team players. How do I know this to be true? Because it happened to me. I trusted the wrong people because I decided to take the wheel from God and guide my own ship right into an iceberg just like the Titanic. My ego had gotten the better of me. Ego - it's a funny thing that ego; it also has a hidden meaning like, ego = edging God out. After I continuously kept losing everything that I owned and the friends I thought were real friends.

I finally woke up to reality - nothing works without God's hand in it. Now, the funny thing here is this: when Jack Williams asked me to run his label sales printing company, I felt God tugging at my heart to do it, but I didn't listen because I had taken the wheel away from him. Instead of listening to God and following my heart, I would change the future that God had planned out for me. He was still wanting to bless me with a shot at becoming a star. In April of 2007, I received a phone call from my adopted stepdad, Jack Williams. God was really trying to get my attention. I wasn't listening, though.

Instead, I chose to stay in Arizona. After my mother kept complaining and constantly badgering me about considering moving back to Dallas, Texas, to help Jack Williams live a better quality of life. Jack was suffering from Parkinson's disease, plus his wife Helen had just died. He said he would not only pay me $500.00 a week to take care of him until the inevitable. He would also make me the beneficiary of his estate. Jack died exactly one year and two months after he called me with his offer. Big mistake on my part.

Had I known that running label sales was actually a backdoor presented to me by God, granting me all access to my dreams, I would have stayed in Dallas, Texas, probably married Beverly, a beautiful red-headed Scottish woman, have four or five children together, and have the acting career God wanted me to have. But I knew best, yeah right, lol. When God speaks, we had better listen.

If we don't, it's crash and burn. A true knight, aka disciple, listens to their wise king. I did not heed the call to leave the city I pretty much grew up in. Every man and every woman must eventually do so to find themselves.

For a prophet cannot excel in his or her own hometown. The greatest man that ever walked the face of this Earth knew it well.

Now go out there, pray to God from your hearts, and most importantly, listen to the voice of wisdom, for true wisdom comes from knowing and knowing comes from God. When I started to manage gentlemen's clubs in Dallas, Texas, in the early nineties, I did it as an experiment to learn something. Why do these women do it? What I learned blew me away, and it also helped me to understand why Tamara, my ex, was doing it. That and the fact that she feared her career opportunities were becoming limited due to her age.

I now understand why she chose to become an exotic entertainer, aka (Stripper). By being on the inside and seeing exactly what they had to put up with - the almost constant creeping hands always trying to grab their ass, or attempts at touching or playing with their areolas, aka nipples, and breasts. I was no longer disappointed or judgmental about her choice. In fact, from that moment on, I even supported her choosing to dance nude. I may not have liked her doing it, but I still supported her decision to do it.

I reasoned with myself that if I could get past this with her, and love and accept her for who she is when she's with me - which meant giving her moral support no matter what - then maybe, just maybe we'd become the team we're supposed to be and work together, build a rock-solid foundation together, and eventually respect one another again.

Well, I was half right anyway. Three months later, Tamara's insecurity started to show after we had just finished making love and getting ready to go work out. After she finished her shower, that's when things changed. She more or less told me to quit my job running the club, saying she didn't trust all those women around me. More like she didn't trust me really. She said it would be fun, and it would also help our relationship to grow.

The old me would have blown my top, started calling her names, and told her how selfish she was. Not today. I was in complete control of my emotions from that day on. You see, I actually could see myself spending the rest of my life with her. However, this was the straw that broke the camel's back, so to speak. Instead, I said, "Honey, don't you think this is a little presumptuous of you? Isn't it kind of unfair to me that you're assuming I want to go to New York and Atlanta,

Georgia with you? I mean, what am I going to do when I get there?"

She smiled, leaned in to kiss me goodbye, and said, "You're going to take care of me, honey. Love you."

I replied, "I love you too, but—"

She stopped me again, put her finger against my lips, and said, "No buts. It'll be like an adventure. Maybe you and I could even do an unknown porno together. We'll just put bags on our heads so no one will know who we are." A porno, really? Which never actually happened, by the way, thank God. Wow, she had already planned this without talking to me. A real team player never does that. Do you see my point?

It gets better. After Tamara had finished her shift at Cabaret Royal that night, she sent me a message on my pager. Here's the message: "Hi honey, I love you. I'm too drunk to drive home. Can you come and pick me up, my special purpose honey? Kiss, kiss, hug, hug."

That was a title she gave me a few weeks after we met in Arizona at Za Zoo's, a once very popular nightclub off 9th Street and Camelback Road in Phoenix, Arizona. I have to admit, she knew how to reel me in. She was everything I ever wanted in a woman until she quit respecting me. Honestly, though, that was my fault because earlier on in our relationship, I had stopped listening to exactly what she was saying.

News flash, guys: if you really love your woman and want to spend the rest of your life with her, marry her. You'd better learn how to really listen, or you will eventually lose her. There was something else I would learn later on about Tamara and what her mother did to her when she was sixteen years old. She put her in a mental institution.

Why, or better yet, how could anyone do that to their own flesh and blood? And yet, in much later years, Tamara forgave her mother. She looked after her, took care of her, until she passed away. Wow, she was one hell of a woman.

In my eyes, that made her an exceptional human being and one hell of a woman. A woman at that point in time I truly wanted to spend the rest of my life with. Unfortunately, we never became that team. I stayed in Dallas, Texas. Continued with my acting classes at The Film Actors Lab with Adam Roarke, and started dating Beverly, the beautiful, sexy Scottish redhead that my friend Charlie introduced me to. I think he planned it, actually.

I'm grateful for it, though. It's an experience I'll treasure for the rest of my life, even though we never got married. Certain moral and ethical obligations regarding my mother and her welfare have had a profound effect on my life. The good thing about it, though, is I'll be prepared when my real partner comes along. This time I'll get it right, for I will know for sure. This time she'll be my lifetime team partner.

This time, it's for keeps, to truly love, honor, and cherish all the days of the rest of our lives. This time I will patiently wait to hear the voice of true wisdom, letting it guide me in the right direction to living a more productive, loving, and fruitful life. That will have a major influence on the people I allow God to put in my path. For a great playwright known by William Shakespeare once said something like this: "Life is but a play and we are all actors gathered upon a stage on which we are to perform."

In other words, after the show is over, and we have lived our lives, wouldn't it be nice to know our lives had a purpose? And we are hopefully remembered for it. We touched their hearts, we made a difference in their lives, even if it was only for a short time. We had fulfilled our purpose by making someone else's life better.

Although assembling a team for anything is important, we must remind ourselves to do it for the right reasons, unselfish reasons. Stop going on social media and posting every time you do a good deed or accomplish something great. There's an old saying, and it still rings true today: loose lips sink ships. Don't let your left hand know what your right hand is doing. Stay focused, wait until it's done, then watch what happens.

Always stay true to others and be true to yourselves. There are way too many fake posers in the world today. Don't allow yourselves to be taken for a ride by all their false promises. And remember, change always starts with you. Become a mentor to a willing recipient; be an example for them. It all starts with one. If you're in your teens or early twenties, I'll say it in a language you understand: remember to always keep it real. And always pray for guidance from our Heavenly Father.

Life was meant to be an adventure, not an obstacle course. So go out there and live your life to the fullest extent. Remember that, in order for you to effectively establish a real group of team players for your job or business and personal relationships, pray and trust in God to bring them to you. That doesn't mean you just sit around all day praying. You have to also be proactive;

you have to take action. For faith without works isn't faith at all.

If we fail to listen to God's instructions and not act on them, then we have a dead faith. For faith without works is dead. If I am wrong, then why does a good father discipline his children? Answer: to teach them right from wrong or what works and what doesn't work, giving them guidance throughout their lives to become and be better human beings.

Now do you see what I mean by finding the right team players? And I'm not talking about playing people to hustle them for money or anything else. I'm talking about establishing a group of people who have strong morals and ethics. Their character isn't flawed or tainted. They want to humbly serve and be of service to others. They freely give of themselves without expecting something in return. They appreciate and reciprocate to those around them. When they're given an increase in their pay, they show genuine appreciation.

By continuing to perform to the best of their abilities, they accept and offer constructive criticism when needed. For how can we fix a problem if we don't see it? These are exactly the kind of moral and ethical people I'd want on my team. Wouldn't you?

It's kind of a real kick in the butt, though, this day and age. Forty years ago, corporate America seemed to follow these moral and ethical guidelines strictly.

Today they don't. What happened? What changed the very life fiber that once drove our economy to be a top-performing country? Where is our "Let's Make America Great Again" mentality? I bet I can tell you the answer in one word: unity. Unity once drove America to not only greatness but the willingness to serve, to lend a helping hand to our neighboring countries.

A real team has to be united in order to thrive and be of service to others. One of the better examples of the true American spirit would be the Guardian Angels, which was founded back in 1979 and has grown and expanded to other cities throughout the United States and other countries throughout the world. Now that's a strong moral and ethical non-violent organization.

Can someone say there's strength in numbers? I know I can.

Chapter 6
Rising Tides of Injustice
Recognizing Systemic Issues and Inequities

After visiting and staying with my mom in Avondale, Arizona, I immediately noticed a major change in the place I once called my hometown, now a big city. Something just wasn't right; this wasn't the same warm and friendly place I pretty much grew up in.

The change was obvious. The people I encountered were really selfish, rude, and obnoxious, not to mention criminal-minded. Gunshots were going off practically every weekend in the once-quiet city of Avondale. Meth heads were constantly walking up and down the block, yelling and screaming all hours of the night, looking for a way to get their next fix.

I witnessed people fighting over stupid, trivial things. Others claimed they didn't get their milk or other grocery products at the local grocers when they clearly took it home and came back to get another one for free. They got away with it for a while as there were no real cameras in the stores back then. This was also costing the American taxpayers more in consumer goods and services.

This was, in fact, the beginning of moral and societal decay. People would always try to get over on the decent people. A new unruly generation was rising up with no moral compass to guide them. Their guide was a PC—not political correctness but a personal computer—with next to no adult supervision. This was part of a mentally immoral product that made things harder on my mom and myself.

With the nosey neighbors always getting into our business and robbing us blind, it was clear this wasn't the neighborhood I grew up in at all. It was like I had stepped into another dimension and wanted to find my way back to the reality of a once sane society. A reality where God was loved, feared, and revered. A reality where morals and ethics were practiced daily. A reality where families got along, prayed together, stayed together, ate dinner and lunch together, sometimes even breakfast, sharing their daily experiences. That reality was now gone.

I told myself it was only temporary after staying there with my mother for two years after I officially left Dallas, Texas, in 1994. I was in the process of breaking up with my ex, Tamara, for good. So I took a job working with a man I considered to be like a father to me, Ken Byrum. Ken spotted me shopping in the grocery store he was managing. Tamara knew that Ken needed my help, especially when he called out my name.

Life was just getting good, right? Wrong. Ken approached us and said, "I thought that was you. Where have you been, son?" I started to introduce him to Tamara, and he then pulled me away from her and said these words, "Dad needs your help, son." This was a man I could never say no to. He had helped me out a lot in the past. Ken walked me through the entire store. In his grocery backroom, there was back stock everywhere. I couldn't believe what I was seeing. Then he said, "You see my problem, son."

I walked along his grocery stock wall and said, "What the hell, Ken? What happened? Your grocery backrooms never looked like this."

He said, "Now it does. It's this political correctness crap. You can't yell at anybody, let alone put the fear of God in them anymore. President Clinton's private little joke on all the baby boomers who still get down and dirty to get the job done—not this generation, though."

"They're all becoming a bunch of pussies." That's when he put his right hand on my shoulder and asked me for help. Tamara had just walked into the grocery backroom. She had daggers in her eyes as soon as she saw me shaking Ken's hand. She knew then that I wasn't going to California with her after all, as I had just made a deal with him. All hell was about to break loose, and it did.

Needless to say, she and I pretty much broke up that week. I worked for Ken for about two months as his night crew manager. I had the grocery backroom organized within three weeks. The shelves were always full and organized under my watch. I was a master at this stuff, and Ken knew it too well. Unfortunately, Ken left that store. It seems that Kevin Durant was so impressed with what I did with Ken's store, he gave him the keys to a better one. Ken was leaving, and I was staying.

For about a month, I stuck it out there. I didn't care for my new boss. He was always running a few hours late just so he could tee off. It seems he really loved to play early morning golf. Ken had told him in advance not to screw with me. Apparently, he failed to listen. It would be the final straw that broke the camel's back. He knew a week in advance that I had to be in Prescott, Arizona, that Saturday by 12:30 that afternoon.

My shift officially ended at 7:30 AM. I waited until 9:30; still no store manager, who was supposed to be in his store by 8:00 AM sharp. He never showed, so I tossed the keys to the morning clerk and said, "You're in charge now. I'm going to be late; I can't be late." Under my breath, I mumbled these words: "I have an acting class to go to." Needless to say, my pager kept vibrating. It was my new boss demanding that I call him back right away. I just kept driving as Prescott was about three hours away from Gilbert, Arizona.

When I returned to work Sunday night at 10:00 PM, as I tapped my key on the glass door, this really young skinny kid unlocked the door and ordered me to punch in. I said, "Who the hell are you, and who made you my boss?" He snickered with sarcasm in his voice and handed me a list of things he expected me to do. I was pissed yet never showed it. I stayed for about thirty minutes, then said to him before I officially decided to go, "Why do you have my keys? What the hell is going on here?"

He looked at me and then said, "Are you staying or leaving?" I left. The following week, I returned to get my last and final check. This was good. Mr. Wannabe golf pro made sure he gave it to me, making his prideful, stupid remarks like this one: "Did you really think you'd win?" I looked him straight in his eyes when he handed me my check.

"I already did. You're the loser for putting an irresponsible kid in a position of authority. You lose; I win."

He said, "How so?"

I said, "It's simple, really. When Kevin Durant realizes that your grocery back room has gone to shit, he's going to want to know why. Have a nice day, loser." Pride always falls before fools. It would do us all well to remember this.

Funny thing about all of this—life really does have a sense of humor. Five weeks later, I would be getting hired on with *Fred Meyer's Foods* as a grocery night stocker, with a cokehead for a grocery manager who thought he was a badass and who also fudged on the inventories by throwing over half of the back stock in the trash compactor. Due to the fact Mike, the store director, threatened to fire Jerry if he couldn't get rid of the back stock, Jerry got rid of it alright and lost the company a lot of money in the process. Jerry was a total asshole who thought his shit didn't stink.

Three weeks later, he was promoted to assistant manager and transferred to a new store. What the hell? This guy stole from the company, didn't get fired, and moved up the corporate ladder by doing everything wrong. Are you serious? Do you not see the significance here? Everything was going backward. People doing really bad things were being treated like royalty, while the ones doing good and right were treated like outcasts, criminals, and villains. The world at this point seemed to have lost its mind.

Justice was eventually served after the two really beautiful twin sisters who worked next door at the pizza place would come over, walking through the store, looking in my direction, waving at me, and smiling. The other guys hated me for this. Richard kept calling me ugly. I knew I wasn't ugly; he was jealous. So was Justin. The only ones who weren't jealous were Robert and Shannon. They remained my friends. I think Shannon may have had a coke problem, though.

Justin was the new grocery manager, who had already decided he didn't like me from the start. He was secretly working on giving my position to his buddy who was moving to Phoenix, Arizona, from Salt Lake City, Utah. Justin was a snake who picked a fight with the wrong guy. He called me into Mike's office to fire me. He was scared shitless when he did it too. As he reached over and hit the terminated button on the computer screen, I made the following comment: He thought I was going to hit him in the face because I jumped up really quickly, literally putting the fear of God into him. As I made this comment with a bit of a smile on my face: "You know, Justin, there are some people in this world you just don't mess with. I'm one of those people—not because I could break your face if I really wanted to, but because I'm a child of God. I'm one of His. And one thing I know is this: God doesn't like for His children to be messed with. I don't know how, I don't know when, but God is going to get you for this because you're areal piece of crap."

Two years later, Justin was riding his brand new Harley Davidson motorcycle he had bought four months ago and got broadsided by a car heading in his direction. My friend Robert told me what happened. This turned Justin into a spoon-fed, full-fledged quadriplegic. He was paralyzed from the neck down. I don't know if this was God or what, but that's why I always treat everyone the way I want to be treated.

I felt bad for Justin, though, knowing he'd never walk again. He was really young, too. The thing is this: if he'd had a crystal ball or some way of knowing that his karma might have contributed to his physical demise, would he have fired me or continued to disrespect others? This we'll never know. But I know this much: he probably remembered that last conversation we had based on his accident.

Speaking of accidents, I was really sad to hear about my older friend Robert's accident slipping off a milk crate, which changed his life forever. This accident could have easily been averted if they had given him easier aisles to stock. By the way, did I mention he was older? He would never have gotten hurt. His quality of life had drastically changed from that moment on.

And *Fred Meyer's Foods* got off cheap. If Robert had listened to me and got his own doctor, he would have had a beautiful case. Instead, he opted for one of their doctors and went with workman's comp insurance. Big mistake. Robert had them by the balls; he just didn't believe it. He got scared and settled. The moral of the story here is this: never settle. Make them pay. Get a lawyer with some strong legal teeth who's not afraid to bite hard, and watch them cave in. You will win in the end. With God on your side, you will always win.

In light of everything happening around me, guess who calls me almost two years later on my pager service?

Yep, Ken Byrum, affectionately known as Dad, wants me to call him right away. Fifteen minutes later, I called him from a pay phone. He asked me how I've been. Apparently, he knew about what happened at Mega Foods. He laughed when I told him the whole story. I found out that the store director had been fired, and Ken no longer worked there.

Ken was now working for Southwest Supermarkets, with Sero running the show from their main corporate office off 20th Street and McDowell Road. I didn't know that at the time. I later found it out after I was hired by the company as their head night stocker, working for Ken again. Again, it was short-lived, about one week this time.

It seems Ken either moved up in the company or quit to go to work for Bashas Foods as an assistant store manager or grocery manager. This kid named Pat took over the Southwest Supermarket that Ken was managing in Goodyear, Arizona. When I say kid, I mean it—hell, he looked like he was seventeen years old. Really, this was my new boss? This guy had zero grocery experience. I believe he once told me he used to manage a Circle K convenience store. What? Are you kidding me? I took two steps backward and put my acting career on hold for this?

I have to admit this, though: in the almost two years I worked there, I never saw him get mad or pissed off. Even though he really didn't know this business, I did respect him as far as treating his employees goes. The one thing I really despised about him the most was his Howdy Doody attitude. Howdy Doody was a fictional character from the late fifties who reprised his role in the late seventies on a TV show that made Henry Winkler a household name. "Happy Days," the show that would officially make him a star.

Now back to Pat. So where was I? Oh yeah, I remember he was always nice and very quickly decided on my word to hire my brother. I knew it was going to be an easy conquest. He didn't even ask any questions about my brother. Hell, I don't even think there was really an interview. Just "Here's the application; fill it out and bring it back. You'll have a job provided your UA (urine analysis) comes back clean."

I still remember that day like it was yesterday. I think Mel was really grateful for what I pulled off. He showed his gratitude in a most loving and profound way. I felt a slight glimmer of hope that this could actually work. It did for four days. Then all hell broke loose. Little did I know about the hell I was about to endure, which led to me getting transferred to a real shithole of a Southwest

Supermarket store that was once located off 51st Avenue and McDowell Road.

Their second worst store in Arizona. The worst was located off 19th Avenue and Buckeye Road. Ken was actually transferred there from Goodyear, Arizona, back in the day. When he left, it really went downhill. This was in the early to mid-nineties. Not only were these the worst of Southwest Supermarkets stores, but they also seemed to always attract employees with criminal minds. If you actually shopped there, you know exactly what I mean.

However, there were some decent people who actually worked in those stores when they were in business. It's a known fact that birds of a feather flock together, meaning they stay together. I hope you're starting to get the picture. I know that Albert Einstein did, and I quote. When asked by a reporter if he feared evil men, his reply was something like this: "I'm not afraid of evil men. What I'm afraid of are the good men who sit idly by and allow the evil to happen. Those are the ones I'm afraid of."

When good men do nothing, evil triumphs. It was never supposed to be this way. So do the right thing when you're driving in your cars. If you see someone committing a crime, record it and report it. There's one crime in particular that goes unreported, and that's texting or surfing social media or the internet on your phone while driving or not moving when the traffic light turns green. Stop it now. These are all crimes, and I'm not talking misdemeanors. I'm talking full-fledged felony offenses.

Texting and driving is six times more likely to cause a car accident than drunk driving and has contributed to over 1.6 million accidents, with numbers increasing every year, based on statistics. This has been continuously happening for almost two decades. It's only getting worse as technology advances.

About ten percent of these are fatal accidents. Because some selfish piece of shit human beings out there obviously have zero respect for other people's right to live, this is the end result. This has to stop. The time has come to prosecute them all to the fullest extent of the law.

Respect the road. Respect the drivers. This ain't no damn video game. You can't press reset. Grow up and act like adults. There is no reset button once you carelessly take someone else's life. If we're going to continue to have a country, we must get back to simplicity. We, as a people, we the people, will not make it if the status quo doesn't change. America, I'm talking to you. Wake up. It's time to become the United States of America again. United we stand; divided we fall.

Your so-called friends, homies, gang members aren't going to save you. Unity will, though. And how about the lazy younger people, and a few older ones, taking advantage of the ones who truly do seventy to eighty percent of the work in the workplace while the rest of you go smoke your pot in the workplace parking lot?

Which actually is a very serious criminal offense. Not to mention very OSHA unfriendly. By the way, if you are addicted to cigarettes and want to smoke, then pick the hell up after yourselves. You can tell a lot about a person's character by the way they act and what they do in and around the workplace.

And let's not forget the weird and unwanted sexual assaults now happening to men from other men who think just because they've been there longer than you, they can grope, grab your ass, talk about your ass, and slide their hand up and down your arm while your bosses stand idly by, watching and laughing, thinking it's funny.

It's not. It's still sexual harassment, especially when you've been asked for over a year to stop it. Now it becomes sexual assault as the individual's response was this: "I can't help myself." For over a year, this guy kept saying this to me.

By the way, this guy was also an alcoholic, former meth head, drug addict, addictive personality, narcissistic jackass, control freak, uneducated piece of work who was always sampling the fruits and vegetables in the DC (Distribution Center). Correct me if I'm wrong, but isn't that called grazing, or let's just call it what it really is —stealing?

Here's what I don't understand: there are people working, doing their job, yet these other worthless bums feel entitled to get on their phones, go smoke a joint in the employee restroom while the supervisors are sitting in a nice warm office because they don't want to get cold.

Hello, they need to get their butts out on the floor, keep an eye on things. That's what a supervisor does. They walk the warehouse floor, just like a police officer walks their beat. It's called a stakeout. Like it or not, that is exactly what they're supposed to do—stake out the warehouse. They refuse to do it because they're getting paid a salary. Really, they made a choice to be a supervisor. It, it's not like somebody put a gun to their head forcing them to take the job.

It's funny, though, as they complain about salary only when they work long hours. Hello, that's what a salary is. What's even more hilarious, though, is the fact that when they work fewer hours, they still get paid for a full week. Who rewrote this rule? If you worked fewer hours back in the eighties and nineties, your salary was prorated to a lesser amount. Do you see the hypocrisy here? How is this right? It's not, actually, because they're not even doing the job for starters. The younger guys they have picking in the warehouse are either working high from smoking pot in the parking lot or buzzing off energy drinks, which is causing them to hit unrealistic numbers.

Compared to the employee who's not getting high, who actually delivered the original rate or performance standard, does the employer even care? What do you think? You tell me. For the days of bosses or corporate America giving a damn about their employees are long gone. There are, however, a few exceptions to the rule here.

When you learn a high-paying, in-demand skill, you are suddenly respected, appreciated, and most of all, never neglected. Why? Because they can't seem to find the people to fill these positions. Apparently, out of the 213,000 to 400,000 available high-skilled jobs throughout the United States, only a few thousand, if even that, of those positions get filled.

Now here's the good news. Even if you have some of these skills, depending on what field it is, they'll usually hire you and train you as an intern or apprentice. As you can see, it becomes a win-win situation for the individual and the employer. Now you're probably wondering how this relates to this chapter. It's simple, really. You see, when you have in-demand skills and your services are needed,

you have successfully started to change the status quo. It may take three to five years to notice it. Believe me, you'll not only notice it, but you'll also be thinking, "Why didn't I learn these skills sooner?" Answer: maybe because of all the electronic distractions we have nowadays. That could be it. No, that is it.

Don't misunderstand me now. Let me make the intention perfectly clear here. We all have one brain, one body with arms, hands, legs, and feet, two eyes, two ears, a nose, teeth, and a tongue. Yet because we are human beings, we usually take all of these for granted. We even tend to abuse them at times without realizing it. For instance, our brains are designed to process one thing at a time.

Multitasking doesn't really work. If it did, then we'd be the most productive nation on this earth. That means no more accidents on the roads because of irresponsible drivers using their phones while driving. Unfinished work would be unheard of. Are you starting to get the picture now? Everything—our sense of smell, our taste buds, our eyes, our hearing—is all connected to the human brain.

How exactly do we then change this all around? Simple: by doing one thing at a time. This in itself will, in fact, change the status quo, which will also help to restore the moral standards of a rapidly decaying society. And always remember to put God first, the one who created it all.

Chapter 7
Heights of Triumph
Victories and Breakthroughs in the Face of Adversity and Setting an Example

Since the beginning of time, mankind has had to learn some hard and often difficult life lessons. Life-changing lessons that would determine whether they would live or die. How did they manage to stay alive? They adapted to their present living conditions, then they innovated by learning what works and what doesn't work.

And then they overcame, meaning they learned how to conquer their attackers. They became the victors simply by following these three things: they watched, listened, and learned. This helped to keep them off the dinner menu. They finally understood that if they confronted their fears instead of running away all the time, they would not only survive, they would thrive.

We have all been there in some way, shape, or form, whether running for our lives or running away from danger. Not all of us will succeed in doing so, but those who do have won a victory. They've successfully gotten away in time; congratulations to them, they're still alive. Because they listened to their intuition, their fight-or-flight response system kicked in. You'll know when it happens: your heart will start beating faster, and your alertness will increase.

And then it happens: you're either fighting for your life or you run like hell to get out of harm's way. In the twenty-first century, if you're not paying attention to all of your surroundings, you could become a target for those looking to either rob you, harm you, or kidnap you, or worse. A very wise man once said this to me: "Watch, listen, and learn, and always be on your guard every time you're out in public. The world has lost its mind."

He wasn't kidding either. Turns out he was right on all counts. When I'm out in public, I don't have my eyes glued to my phone. I don't even have my phone out. I keep my phone in my pocket, set on vibrate, just in case I get a call. I'm always looking around, observing my environment to avert any potential violent or dangerous situations. I never let my emotions get in the way of my judgment in any situation. At the same time, I'm always looking for an opportunity to help those who are in true need of some assistance.

I used to see a lot of people doing this years ago; not anymore. Society has become emotionally ratchet. It thinks of doing one thing and one thing only: making money. Apparently, they're not interested in helping their fellow man out of the goodness of their hearts. Athletes used to play sports because they loved doing it. Now we have a bunch of out-of-shape posers trying to act like real athletes.

This is, of course, my own personal opinion, yet the evidence shows I may be right. Just compare today's athletes with the athletes of the seventies, eighties, and nineties; there's no comparison. They were stronger, faster, and had high endurance and focus. They even gave back to society, especially one former NFL player who played for the Arizona Cardinals from Phoenix, Arizona.

His name was Pat Tillman, a man who was a true champion in every sense of the word. A true American who showed us he not only loved his family and country, but he also appreciated and respected what it stood for. So much so that on April 22, 2004, he was killed in action by friendly fire.

He gave up everything simply because he knew in his heart it was time to give something back. God rest his soul. His legacy will continue on for many years to come. Pat Tillman was and always will be a real champion. And then there's my good friend, Randall McDaniel.

We used to work out in the same weight training room at Agua Fria Union High School. A man with a heart of gold that I always knew was going to become a football star. In 1988, he was handpicked after surviving the Minnesota Vikings' first-round draft pick as a fierce guard. From 1990 to 1999, for the Minnesota Vikings, he finished 14 seasons.

He left the Vikings and signed on with the Buccaneers from 2000 to 2001, completing 12 pro bowl starts. He eventually would become a teacher after leaving the NFL. He believes wholeheartedly in giving back. He is not only a shining example of what a positive role model means to these young teenagers, but he's also a true champion in every sense of the word. Thank you, Randall, for making a difference in these young teenagers' lives.

Today's athletes don't even seem to be into doing that. They're only interested in one thing, and that's money.

Real athletes are not. They're not only competitive, they're noble, brave men of honor, positive role models whom the youth used to look up to and model themselves after.

Nowadays, they honor athletes—questionable athletes—with a gangster thug mentality. Is this really what we want for our younger generation? God, I hope not. Enough is enough. It's sad that humanity has digressed this way. There's an old saying: if it ain't broke, don't fix it. Well, this society is broken; it's been broken for a long time. It's time to fix it now.

And then there are the so-called genius online business gurus. Ninety-five percent of them don't even know what they're talking about. They want payment to help or assist those in need, so they say, as they so cleverly try to disguise it. On their social media platforms, they use phrases like this: "I want to help you get rich in six months, or sixty days, sometimes even less."

And then they hit you with some ridiculous one-time payment of $997.99, or a so-called monthly affordable payment plan of $225.95 for four months. They're hoping you'll buy into their money-making scam, even if you don't have it. So where and when did it all go wrong? It started with the families that stopped eating together and praying together.

Then TV, then the public schools, and finally the computer and cell phones. We are all being hypnotized into believing it's fun to laugh at someone when they fail or fall. This isn't normal; it's sick and twisted. If you see someone fall, don't laugh at them. Lend them a hand, help them up. Help them succeed when they fail simply by giving them moral support.

What happened to doing the right thing? Society is caught up in chasing success, becoming rich; they've forgotten about the simple things in life: God, family, and friends. The things that really make a difference, the things that really matter. But look what the system has created: a bunch of misguided, ill-informed people who can't even take care of themselves, looking to either hit the lottery or invest in some off-the-wall get-rich-quick scheme. Instead, they should be focusing on God and praying to Him for guidance to give them what they need, not what they want.

Now, I know what you're thinking: what does any of this have to do with victory and being triumphant? It has everything to do with it. Think of it like this: if a true champion is going to prevail and become victorious, first he must see it in his mind's eye. Then he must train really hard to prepare his body and mind for the fight of his life. That fight is to win the game or event he or she is competing in.

In today's world, it appears that society has either forgotten how to do this or they simply don't care anymore. The competitive spirit seems to have died. Parents and schools are giving their children ribbons and trophies just for trying. What on God's green Earth are they doing?

Don't they realize that giving ribbons, awards, and trophies just because they tried is a recipe for disaster? With no real goal setting in their lives at all, especially after their children hit a certain age. Instead of setting goals and reaching for the stars, they expect the world to cater to them. Their parents might not know it yet, but they're setting them up to fail.

It's important for the parents to understand that they must always create and set goals for their children to accomplish. This, in turn, will give them a sense of purpose. A competitive spirit is actually healthy to have. It not only builds up your confidence and self-esteem, it actually builds up your character.

This in itself is a major victory in defining who you are and what you wish to become. So parents, please stop giving your children consolation ribbons, awards, and trophies just for trying. Last I looked, there were only three winners in a competition: 1st, 2nd, and 3rd. That's it. There are no consolation trophies or ribbons. Make them earn it.

If you don't, you're actually programming them into believing all they have to do is try half-assedly and opportunity will come knocking. This is not true. It will make them become complacent, lazy, video game-playing, junk food-eating kids in adult obese-sized bodies, vaping, doing stupid things, getting high in the parking lot where they work, working a job they actually hate, and doing more stupid things, not giving a damn how they do the job at all.

Congratulations, you just set your kids up to fail. You've also set a very bad example by rewarding them for doing half-assed work with the mindset of "it's good enough; that's all that counts." Sorry, but good enough isn't good enough. That's not going to cut it in the real world. In the real world, you don't try, you do. A loser tries one time, but a winner never quits. They continue going until they win. Now let me make something perfectly clear here.

I'm not saying don't try. What I'm saying here is don't give up. Keep trying; you will eventually win. I've personally met and known real-life Super Bowl champions from the eighties and nineties. The difference between them and the players today is simple. They put their hearts into it. I don't see the players in today's game doing that. I see a bunch of mid-grade, overpaid, out-of-shape wannabe champs.

I was actually approached by a 49ers football coach back in 1985 to try out for their first-round draft picks. I was a part-time busboy working in the restaurant of a hotel that was known as the Grand Inn. I politely declined the offer because I had other obligations that needed to be taken care of at the time. Seven years later, in Lewisville, Texas, at a country and western nightclub that Jimmy Johnson, a very well-known former Dallas Cowboys coach, would sometimes go to, another opportunity presented itself when I was doing some dancing on the dance floor.

Apparently, Mr. Johnson was so impressed with my performance on and off the dance floor that he personally asked me to sit down and have a drink with him. Which I did. He then told me, "That was one hell of a move you did out there, son. Where'd you learn to move like that?"

I started to explain to him where and how, and then he stopped me. He replied with this: "Son, do you know who I am?"

"You're Jimmy Johnson; everybody knows who you are."

He then said this to me: "How would you like to try out for the Dallas Cowboys' first-round draft picks? They're starting in three weeks. I can get you in. What do you say?"

I was completely speechless for about ten seconds. Then I replied, "Mr. Johnson, I don't know what to say."

He said, "All you gotta do is just say yes." He continued, "I believe you might even have the potential to become an MVP, a star. I'll start you out making thirty-five thousand a year. You'll travel, see the country. I'm gonna need you to gain about sixty-five more pounds, though."

I said, "Sixty-five more pounds? I already weigh around two hundred and twenty pounds."

He then explained to me why he wanted me to gain sixty-five more pounds, told me I would be trying out for a defensive end position. I then very tactfully interrupted him and told him that I made more than thirty-five thousand a year. He asked how much more. I said, "Around twenty thousand more."

He smiled, then continued his pitch: "Did I forget to mention that we also pay you a per diem? And we provide the best gyms for our players to work out in."

He then extended his right hand for me to shake it, expecting me to do the same. When I didn't, he realized my answer was going to be either "thank you, but no thanks," or just "no thank you." I gotta hand it to Jimmy, though. Even after I said no, he reached over, put his right hand on my left shoulder, and said these words: "Why? I gotta know, why are you going to turn down a once-in-a-lifetime opportunity that most guys would kill for?"

Then I responded with this: "Joe Montana had a long NFL career, and he was a quarterback."

He replied, "Yes, he did, and he was a great quarterback. But what's that got to do with you?"

"I'm getting to that."

He then said, "Okay," and gestured for me to continue.

Which I did. "In his long career, what happened to his back, his legs, his knees? There's no amount of money that's ever going to be able to fix the physical problems his body is having now, not to mention the pain he now has to live with and deal with for the rest of his life."

You see, deep down inside, I knew I had what it takes to make it in the NFL. So did Jimmy. He immediately knew I did based on the way I handled myself that night. He wanted one more victory before he retired. I believe that he believed I could have given him that victory if I actually would have gone to the first-round draft picks. And now back to our story.

Jimmy responded with these words: "I see your point, but we can't live our lives in fear."

Then I replied with this: "True, but we can't live our lives in constant, enduring physical pain either."

This time he smiled and said something like this: "I have never met anybody like you in my life." He then extended his right hand again. We shook hands and parted ways. That was the first and last time I ever personally ran into him. I gotta admit it, though. After personally meeting and talking with him, if I had decided at that time in my life to try out for the NFL and make the grade, I would have gladly signed on with the Cowboys simply because they proved to be real champions back in the nineties. At a time when the competition was fierce, the players actually played because they loved the game, and the destination was also one hell of a ride. Nothing like the media circus we all have witnessed on the football fields in the twenty-first century.

We want to believe that the players are giving us one hundred percent genuine performances, but they're obviously not. It's like going out to a movie theater and paying for a very pricey seat to see a movie that isn't even worth watching. Not so much because the story sucked, but because it wasn't the story that actually sucked. It was the actors that sucked. When a lot of people are getting up to go buy popcorn and soft drinks at the movies, that's usually a sign the BS meter just went off. By the way, BS is short for bullshit. Are you starting to get the picture now?

I'll say it in one sentence: real heroes don't sell bullshit to the ones who look up to them. They deliver one hundred percent. That's why they're heroes. They won't stop until they've won a victory for the people. Because they're true, noble, and valorous men, and in some situations, even noble and valorous women.

Who have actually found their purpose in life, their reason for being. Now, what do you think would happen if the younger generations actually put in the real work to find their purpose? The answer may surprise you if you're in your late teens to early forties. If you're older than that, you probably already know where I'm heading with this. If not, you soon will. For now is the time for us to change the status quo.

You'll begin to instantly recognize what you need to be doing versus what you need to stop doing. This, in turn, will steer you right into the direction of your purpose. Congratulations, you've just won a major victory on your narrow road of purpose. Which in time you will become a triumphant warrior. Who will not only protect your loved ones' and friends' best interests, but you'll also protect their honor as well.

It's very disturbing and hard for any of us nowadays to navigate through all the advancing technology. AI, social media platforms, without feeling a little or a lot overwhelmed. We've become so engrossed in relying on technology and social media so much that it's slowly starting to control all of our lives. It's up to mankind to stop this insanity from growing like mold fungus. We must enact a collective action now, put on the brakes, in order to become triumphant and win a major victory over technology.

We control it, not it controlling us. If we become a complacent (comfortable) society, then humanity is doomed! Technology, AI, social media, governments—

all win, and we lose. We must never allow this to happen. Nothing is ever free in this world. Everything and everyone has a price. The question is, are we willing to pay the price?

In the movie, "The Karate Kid," Mr. Miyagi appears to be taking advantage of young Daniel by having him wash and wax the car, paint the fence, and sand the floor. After thirteen lessons, Daniel finally understands. He realizes that Mr. Miyagi was not only teaching him karate but also discipline and muscle memory. This ultimately brings him victory in the martial arts tournament, the admiration of the girl, and a really cool car. Not because they were owed to him, but because he earned them. He wasn't afraid to pay the price.

He knew from the beginning that he had to act soon, or the wolves would eat him alive. He chose not to be a victim but a victor instead. None of us, especially men, should ever become victims of circumstances beyond our control. We must always protect our women, children, family, and friends. There is a champion in all of us waiting to emerge, but only if you sincerely want it to. You first have to earn the right to be a champion.

How do you do that? With discipline, commitment, and focus. It all comes down to one thing: how badly do you want it? I'll give you one more example. When I was sixteen, I made a commitment to myself and my older brother that nobody would ever use me as a punching bag or disrespect me again. I trained hard all summer. When school started, my peers noticed my physical transformation and something else—confidence. I was beaming with it, so much so that even the most popular girls noticed me. This happened because I paid the price. Most people today aren't willing to pay the price. That's too bad for them; they'll never know true victories. No pain, no gain. Do yourself a favor—don't join their club; it will only drain you. Misery loves company! Don't be their company.

Always set the bar high, no matter what your goal is. Make sure you always play fair, and never settle for second best. And one more thing, and this is crucial: when you're working out at the gym (and yes, it is a gym, not a fitness center—there's a big difference), you must make a commitment to your workout. In a gym, you take only a 30-45 second rest between sets, causing the muscle to contract. This doesn't happen in a fitness center. Most members of so-called fitness centers spend more time on their phones than working out. They might as well go home, binge-watch Netflix, and stuff their faces with pizza. Yes, this might bruise some egos, but it needed to be said. Political correctness is not only destroying society but also truth. So, here's some truth to help us get back on the physical fitness track and make America beautiful again. It starts in the gym.

And please, for God's sake, don't believe everything you hear and see on the Internet, especially on social media. Use your brain—go to the library archives and conduct thorough research. You may be surprised by what you find. Real information is powerful when used in its full context. It empowers us and others like this: when you first learned to crawl, you eventually learned to walk, then run, and finally ride a bike. All that time, believe it or not, you were in training. After learning all of this, you triumphed over adversity. It's in your DNA; it just needed a little help from your parents to come out.

You see society was never meant to fail. Political propaganda, media, and social media bombard us with negative input, making us feel inadequate. Whether they realize it or not, that's questionable. So, let us look at the facts. According to the U.S. Census Bureau in 2022, approximately 18.3 million children across America live without a father in the home, comprising about 1 in 4 children throughout the United States. That number is much higher now. How did this happen?

I believe the answer is God. Ever since life began, we've faced challenges and learning stages that define our character. Everything we've tried or accomplished is now out in the open for the world to see. People will either say great things about you after you pass away, or they'll say nasty things. It happens all the time; people either love you or hate you.

In the fictional tale *A Christmas Carol* Scrooge, a very rich and selfish old man, is granted a gift to see his future for three nights. On the third and final visit from the Spirit of Christmas Future, he discovers that he is loathed and hated. After seeing his name on the headstone, he begs the spirit for another chance, realizing the error of his ways. Luckily for Scrooge, he wakes up on Christmas morning with a new outlook on life. He becomes born again with a renewed hunger to serve mankind, granted the opportunity to change his life story. He showed the world a repentant heart and soul. He made a conscious decision to change.

Even though this story is fictional, it has significance. Charles Dickens, the creator of that story, could have succeeded in any field he chose. He was a strong-minded man who set goals for himself, writing fifteen fictional novels. Thank God he did, or the world would have been cheated out of great stories of triumph and victory. Yet, at the same time, he broke through to our hearts and made people.

Society needs to start thinking for itself again. The hour of repentance is upon us. It's either sink or swim; hopefully, you want to swim. Nobody wants to drown, right? If your ship is sinking, you grab a life jacket and jump off. Life often plays out this way in personal, spiritual, and business relationships.

We often make wrong choices based on feelings and emotions, which get in the way of better judgment. Especially today, we're like millions of AI robots walking in circles with no real destination. Due to a lack of positive role models or mentors, many turn to the Internet for answers. The Internet, a virtual world, started being developed in 1955. But why was it created? What is its true intention regarding the welfare of the world today? Is it honorable or dishonorable? That's the $500 trillion dollar question: are they looking to help society or conquer it?

The good news is we don't have to buy into all the social media dogma. It's an illusion created to test our willpower. You might wonder who I am to make such profound statements about social media and why I'm doing it. The answer is simple: don't get caught up in the social media matrix. It's like a matrix because things aren't always what they appear to be. Just like in the movie *The Matrix* nothing was ever the same after he took the red pill. The veil was removed, and true reality was exposed. Just like in *Alice in Wonderland,* where Dorothy's little dog pulled back the curtain to expose the truth, reality finally steps in, and Dorothy wakes up

It's time to wake up and smell the coffee. Stop responding to trolls on social media. Most of those accounts are either fake or AI bots. The social media platforms are a sneaky way of peeking into the human psyche. It's like stepping into another dimension of sight and sound, but it's not real—we can't touch it, hold it, smell it, or taste it. It's a virtual matrix designed to emotionally enslave us, seeking approval with likes, hearts, thumbs up, or thumbs down. It's like we're experimental lab rats seeking daily doses of dopamine. If we don't get the approval we want, our dopamine levels fall, and we become addicted to social media.

We must rise up and become conscious of what's happening to ourselves, our families, and society. We need to develop the discipline to get off this addiction train called social media. Make a commitment to use it only for business needs and occasionally to check on friends. It's okay to like a comment or respond with constructive criticism. Think before you type.

However, it isn't okay to attack others with words (even on social media) simply because you disagree. That's what a child would do, not an adult. So here's some friendly advice: stop attacking others and start respecting their opinions. After all, we're all adults here, aren't we?

Chapter 8
Descending into Darkness
Navigating Through Personal Struggles and Setbacks: The Toll of Heroism on the Human Spirit

When my father died, I knew it would be one of the most difficult times in my teenage life. With only six and a half weeks left of summer and continuously hearing the echo of my Uncle Buddy's voice in my head, I began to slowly notice what was happening to our family and what would eventually happen to me. I realized how my life would continue to change based on honor and respect, which I believed in then and still do to this day. Without honor and respect, we are nothing.

It would be these beliefs and my family that would cause me to lose everything I ever owned. I even lost myself at my lowest points in life. What I didn't realize was that this wasn't really a loss at all. This was breaking me into becoming the man I needed to be to get through the wilderness. Just like gold, I was being forced into the fire and forged into becoming the man I needed to be. This was my University of Life—the University of Hard Knocks.

I wasn't bitter anymore for the things my family had done to me or how they treated me. I even came to the realization that maybe, unconsciously, I may have unknowingly provoked them in some way, shape, or form. If that is indeed the case, then I wholeheartedly apologize for doing so.

I would often think about it when I had to walk all the way from Avondale to Scottsdale, Arizona, which I did three times due to a lack of funds and transportation from extenuating circumstances beyond my control at the time. I knew I could do it, as I had walked from Westchester, California, all the way to Van Nuys, California, back and forth for three days straight.

A friend of my roommate, who was a regular stand-in for lead actors and also a SAG background actor, apparently got my information from Cenex Casting. According to my roommate and good friend at the time, Don Bisbee, his buddy told him he got me a job on a major film set as a stand-in for Chazz Palminteri. The film starred Sean Penn, Kevin Spacey, Chazz

Palminteri, and Robin Wright Penn. I said, "Sorry, but I can't do it."

He then said, "You have to. Plus, you're going to get three SAG vouchers for doing it, which means you'd be eligible to join SAG. I'm going to be working on two other films for about three weeks. I already told them you'd do it!"

This guy was a real piece of work. After he said that, he abruptly left our apartment. I told Don, "I don't have my truck anymore, remember? It was stolen. If you can take me to the set for those three days, I'll pay you gas money and buy you lunch on Friday."

He said, "I can't. Char is expecting me to be in Tracy for the next four days." Don then went upstairs to take a shower. But before he did, he acknowledged that his friend should have actually asked me before making a commitment on my behalf.

I was pissed! So, I went for a little walk to help me think it through. During my walk, I remembered when I had walked from Irving, Texas, to downtown Dallas back in 1993 after my 1989 Nissan pickup broke down on me between Grapevine and Irving, Texas, around 4:00 AM. I was heading back to my apartment in North Dallas, which didn't happen. I assessed the situation, grabbed my gym bag, and changed into my gym clothes. Thank God I had forgotten to put them in my apartment earlier.

I then rolled up my suit to help avoid it getting wrinkled, locked up my truck, and started walking to downtown Dallas to make my ten o'clock audition. I actually arrived there at 9:25 AM. This gave me plenty of time to find a restroom, get cleaned up, and use the handicapped stall to change back into my suit as the audition called for a business suit. Everything went beautifully. I even came in with my gym bag, which I left by the door. Apparently, they were so busy that they didn't even notice it. After the audition was over, I felt confident that something good was going to happen because I didn't hear those dreaded words every actor fears: "Thank you very much, we'll be in touch," which usually means you're not going to get the part. Instead, they kept asking me questions like, "Where did you study?" and "How long have you been an actor?"

I sincerely and respectfully answered all their questions. After that, we shook hands. They said it was a pleasure meeting me and hoped to be shooting the commercial soon. Bingo, baby! My ship was finally coming in. The commercial in question just happened to be a national commercial. Nothing was going to stop me now. An hour later, I received a phone call from my agent. She congratulated me on getting the job.

I was speechless, then said, "When are they shooting it?"

She said, "I don't know yet. They're going to call me back with all the details." I thanked her for getting me the audition, then walked a few more miles down Greenville Avenue, stopped at a convenience store (I think it was a *Seven-Eleven*), and had just enough money to buy a Big Gulp to celebrate my getting the commercial.

Unfortunately, my celebration didn't last long. Twenty minutes later, after walking down to the Tom Thumb off of Lovers Lane, my agent called my PageNet pager service again. This time the message said, "Sorry, kiddo, the investors pulled the plug on the commercial spot. Better luck next time." I was crushed. How could I be on top of the world less than an hour ago and then come crashing down twenty minutes later?

After that, I walked from downtown Dallas to Las Colinas to make my scene study class at The Film Actors Lab. I did make it, even arriving early. My teacher and mentor, Adam Roarke, noticed I was dripping wet. He looked out the window—not a cloud in sight, not even any rain. He asked me how I got so wet.

When I shared my story with him, he couldn't believe how motivated I was. Not even Lou had ever done anything like that. After reflecting on that past experience in Texas, I knew that if I didn't go, I would probably never get another acting job in L.A. again. Plus, the SAG vouchers, which I never got, were my key motivation. In the end, the producers didn't honor our agreement, but I held up my end, even if it meant walking all the way to Westchester for three days straight, back and forth. I was determined to do it. I paid a really high price for doing it, though. After the third and final day of shooting, walking back to Van Nuys, as soon as I hit the Van Nuys city limits, my legs started convulsing.

As I finally got to our apartment, I started to shake like I was cold, even though I wasn't. I couldn't stop shaking. Luckily for me and my legs, Don walked through the door twenty minutes later. Apparently, he got a call from his agent for an audition and left Tracy early to make it. Thank God he did, as my shaking and convulsions were getting worse. Don couldn't believe I had walked all the way from Westchester and back to Van Nuys for three consecutive days.

Don knew exactly what to do from his former military experience. I believe he was once in the Navy. It took about three hours of me sitting in a tub filled with ice and enduring the pain and shaking convulsions to get my muscles to relax. My muscles had tensed up from all the walking. My leg muscles were in shock. Around 8:30 PM, they finally stopped convulsing. They still hurt, though, and it took about two days of bed rest for the pain to go away. No matter how dark and bleak a situation looks, we can still overcome it. If I can do it, what's your excuse?

With everything that I had gone through, as well as things I would eventually go through in the future, I still held a certain level of respect from people who truly knew me and my character. I still believed in right and wrong, or if you prefer, what works versus what doesn't work. If it wasn't for my loving grandmother, who always took the time to listen to me and share her wisdom, I probably would have turned out differently.

To this day, I thank God for Grandma Vaughn. She was also my godmother. She had a feisty Southern Baptist spirit and eventually decided to become Catholic. She had a way of getting me to see the light in any situation. She always told me to keep my eye on the ball. It took me until I turned thirty years old to finally grasp exactly what that meant. It means to never settle, stay focused on your goals with the end result already in sight.

Which I did after I turned thirty. For the first time in my life, I knew exactly what I wanted to do, where I was headed, and how I would eventually get there. The biggest thing that eventually put the brakes on my plan would be my nosy neighbors and my family. Apparently, my mother had been bragging about the famous and powerful people I was meeting and establishing a strong rapport with.

Not to mention the fact that I was showing positive signs of moving up in the world, even though I asked her not to share my personal information with anyone, including the neighbors, especially the neighbors. Unfortunately, she continued to brag about me. She even told them I was going to be a Chippendale dancer, which was incorrect.

What I said was that I had a shot at becoming a Chippendale dancer if I wanted it. At the time, they wanted me to audition for Chippendales. I said no thank you when they told me how much they were going to pay me. Yep, that's what I said. Yet somehow, everything got lost in translation, so much so that even my cousins were telling their friends and work colleagues that I was a Chippendale dancer.

Maybe a dancer, but not a Chippendale dancer. I have a theory on this, though. Maybe my mother believed that if the neighbors knew I was really close to success as a Chippendale dancer (of which I never was one), I would eventually become a leading man on the silver screen. That maybe they would support me as well. They didn't. They mocked me, saying I didn't know certain people my mother had shared information about. They became envious and jealous of me.

Every chance they got, they would talk shit about me, spreading negative energy into my life. How's that, you ask? Loose lips sink ships, that's how. People today are playing the fool when they share everything they're working on with the world by putting it up on social media. Indirectly, whether they realize it or not, they're allowing people to see into their future plans for success.

Then, someone makes a comment about what they posted. Now the person who willingly shared their information with the world responds with this crap. Sorry, but it is crap. Haters are gonna hate! Congratulations, you just set the stage for failure. Now, all that negative energy is going to eventually come back at you in full force. You'll probably eventually lose everything you've got, including your self-respect.

The lesson: think before you type it. Pay close attention to everything you're posting. Don't take the bait and end up getting into a political discussion. Believe it or not, there's always some form of politics involved. And lastly, always treat others the way you want to be treated. Which brings me to this point: if you don't want to end up penniless (aka with no money at all), then don't air your business all over social media.

If you don't give them any real information and they know very little to nothing about your personal goals, then they can't hurt you with their negative energy. Grandma used to say, "Don't let your left hand know what your right hand is doing." She also said, "Mind your own business." I love you, Grandma. I really miss our talks.

My grandmother, unfortunately, passed away in 1994. She apparently didn't realize just how wise she was, but I did. After I almost died from walking pneumonia in the winter of 1988—it certainly felt that way at the time—if it wasn't for my grandmother, I probably wouldn't be here today.

In the winter of 1987, I would come to understand, at one of the darkest times in my life, just how wise my grandmother was. Remember I told you I lost everything? Well, that wasn't exactly everything—not yet, anyway. My ex-wife, who I found out later on by the end of that year, wasn't really my wife. It seems that the judge who married us, a friend of hers, said he could marry us but apparently never sent in the marriage license to the county records office.

I felt deceived, hustled in some way, but he assured me I wasn't. He told me the whole story about why our marriage wasn't even a marriage. It was because he had been suspended from the bench based on alleged accusations made against him. That's why he decided to open up his bail bonds business. This would also become a blessing in disguise in the not-too-distant future.

Tamara came over to my studio apartment, which was located off 40th Street and Camelback Road, to talk. Well, the talking turned into her yelling at me and me attempting to calm her down, which only made her more pissed off. She picked up the knife that was lying in the kitchen sink and started chasing me around the apartment with it. I had forgotten to close the blinds, and one of the neighbors apparently saw her chasing me with the knife and called the police.

When the police knocked on my door, Tamara went to peek out through the security peephole. Before opening the door, she looked back at me with a sinister smile and said, "You're going to jail." Due to the fact I had to punch her in the chest, it wasn't assault; it was self-defense. I pulled the punch, and I warned her in advance that if she didn't put the knife down, I would have to take it away by force. That's when I realized one of the neighbors witnessed the whole thing. When the cops came in, they immediately started to apprehend her.

Little did I know that even after I decided not to press charges against Tamara for coming at me with a knife, the two Phoenix police officers who answered the 911 call strongly suggested I do it. I decided not to after hearing Tamara out. They had her pinned down on the right side of my bed, getting ready to cuff her. I said, "Let her go." They did, and I wouldn't hear from her for almost two months.

She called me and said she wanted to talk to me. I then drove over to Forget Me Knot's, our antique store/refinishing company. She talked, all right. For almost an hour, she berated and belittled me. It was horrible, but I took it because that's what a man is supposed to do, right?

Then, for no apparent reason, she said something like, "I'm hungry."

I said, "I'm not."

She then said, "What's wrong with you?" She was quiet for about three seconds, then said, "Well, I'm going to Carl's Jr. I'd like some company if you don't mind. I don't like to eat alone." I decided it was in both our best interest to go. So I went with her. We ordered our food. She smiled, even kissed me. A sigh of relief came over me. I truly loved this woman; that's why she had the power to hurt me.

Maybe it wasn't her true intention to hurt me, which she did. I still believed that after not pressing charges against her when I could have, she would hopefully wake up to the fact of just how much she meant to me. After we finished eating, she invited me over to her apartment, which I signed for, due to the fact that she had really bad credit. To show her just how much I loved her and wanted to honor her and keep her and her family safe.

I finally felt like we'd broken through a wall. Her guard was actually coming down, at least, it seemed that way. What I didn't realize was that Tamara, even though she was 15 years older than me, had never really dealt with her demons. I was learning how to deal with mine, which is pretty normal for a 24-year-old male. Tamara was 39 years old when we met. She didn't look it, though. She was everything I'd ever wanted in a woman, at least she appeared to be.

At that point in my life, while I was working on a film set in Scottsdale, Arizona, Tamara had gotten involved in a sexual relationship with a former customer of ours. She thought I didn't know, but I did. I could see it every time he mysteriously just popped into our shop. He was a former cop who owned a security surveillance company known as Security Specialists. His company catered mostly to high-profile people. John happened to be on the same set I was actually working on as an extra cast member that day.

Tamara actually called me to let me know that John was going to be on the same film set with me that day. She also asked me if I had keyed his black limousine. I said no; she didn't believe me, though, neither did John. Until I personally went up to him and said this: "If Tamara really wants to be with you, I'm okay with that."

John then said, "It doesn't make any sense. I was ready to kick your ass for keying my limousine." He knew at that moment it wasn't me.

I was starting to realize that maybe she would be better off with someone like John. He was rich, drove a Porsche. I think one of his neighbors was Senator John McCain. He looked at me and said, "You really do love her, don't you?" I shook my head yes, then he said, "I'm pretty much done with her anyway. If you really want her, you can have her." I was mortified and pissed off by his response. I couldn't believe what I was hearing. I really thought they were in love with one another.

After the shoot was over and we all went home, I received a phone call a few hours later from Tamara on my pager service asking me to please call her right away. I did. She told me that John told her everything I said. I then said, "I'm glad he did. And I meant every word of it." She was suddenly very quiet. In that eerie, awkward quiet moment, I started to say, "I love you. I'll never stop loving you," with a brief pause, then continued with, "Goodbye to her for good."

She very abruptly interrupted me and said this: "Who the hell do you think you are, handing me off like some used car to John?" I was speechless. I just listened in awe. I thought that was the right thing to do. Isn't it written somewhere out there that if you love someone, set them free? Finally, she said, "The next time you feel the need to hand me off like an old dish towel, don't." Then she said, "Where are you right now?"

I said, "I'm at my apartment."

She said, "I want to see you tonight. Can you drive over here?"

I said, "Yes." She asked how long it would take me to get there. I replied, "About twenty minutes."

She said, "Make it fifteen. I really want to see you. I love you."

I said, "I love you too." So I got in my fully dressed T-top black and gold trimmed Chevrolet Camaro and headed over to the Tamaron Apartments in Tempe. When I got there, Tamara answered the door. She was wearing pink lace transparent, very sexy lingerie. She extended her hands to me, kissed me passionately, then slapped my face.

She then grabbed my chin and said, "Listen here, buddy. If I decide that I'm done with our relationship, that's the only way I'm leaving. You don't get to hand me off to the highest bidder, so to speak." She then started to cry and said something like this: "I'm not some used rag doll you can just toss around, honey. I'm a woman with feelings, who happens to be in love with you. I've decided to be in your life, and neither you nor John Hobson are going to hand me off like a pair of used shoes. I love you, not John."

Our relationship was finally heading in the right direction. For almost three months, it was total bliss. We went out to the movies like we did when we started dating. I remember that earlier in December of 1986, she talked about wanting to see *Heartbreak Ridge,* starring Clint Eastwood and Mario Van Peebles. Apparently, she knew Clint Eastwood from the Playboy Club in Phoenix, Arizona, where she worked. She even had pictures of her and her girlfriend sitting next to Clint Eastwood along with some other cast members on a bench.

Through most of the movie, she kept sharing more information about her working in a few of Eastwood's movies, even a Western. Then, from out of the blue, she said this: "I could probably arrange for you to meet with him in the future if you're interested."

I said, "Really? Just like that?"

She said, "No, it wouldn't be just like that. First, I'd have to contact my good friend John Quade. He played a lot of villain roles in quite a few of Clint's movies."

I smiled and said, "Okay, sounds good."

She never called John to set up an introduction for me to officially meet him or Clint. I knew she knew him based on all the photos she shared with me of him and her on movie sets. And a few that I believe may have actually been taken at her former residence on Cholla Street in Paradise Valley, Arizona. I think maybe she didn't do it because she thought I might embarrass her in some way. Or fear got the better of her, thinking I would more than likely be leaving her once my acting career took off.

I knew very little about John or Clint at the time until I met Tamara. The only thing I knew about them was what I learned from watching their movies at the Oasis Drive-in in Avondale, Arizona, when I was a kid. I was actually blessed by the information she shared with me about both of them. Mostly good information about both of them. They were both very talented men and still are today. Unfortunately, John Quade died on August 9, 2009. Rest in peace, John Quade.

Tamara and my relationship were over long before he died. I officially left Tamara for good after New Year's Day of 1995. After she called me and wished me a happy new year, it was officially over, and she finally knew it. Three months later, she took my truck. Apparently, when you co-buy, not co-sign, you can legally do that. All because I got invited to go to Santa Fe, New Mexico, to meet and read for some well-known casting directors in March of that year.

Which cost me a little over $200.00 at the time, making the payment on the truck four days late. Like a thief in the night, she sent her new love interest to come and get it. I ended up walking from 59th Avenue and Bell Road all the way back to my mom's house in Avondale, Arizona. It took me five hours to get there.

The worst part would hit me when I went to purchase a brand new 2000 fully loaded Nissan Frontier based on my 700 credit score from two months ago. I was filled with excitement; the tables appeared to be turning in my favor. When I arrived at the dealership on Grand Avenue in Glendale.

I already knew what I wanted. The salesman was very helpful. I told him what my credit score was. He said with a score of 700, we should have you in that truck and out of here within about thirty to forty-five minutes max. I shook his hand, and we went inside. I filled out the paperwork, and they ran my credit. Ten minutes later, he came back with this: "Mr. Knight, I have some bad news. Apparently, your ex-wife Tamara Davis surrendered the Nissan pickup you and she co-bought five or six years ago exactly two months ago."

Hell hath no fury like a woman scorned. I knew that because I was no longer with her and refused to bow down to her controlling and manipulative ways. She found one way to let me know she was still in charge. By defaulting on the last payment to pay off the loan, she was going to teach me a lesson. What was even more puzzling was the fact that exactly one month after she surrendered the pickup, she paid it off. I don't really know if she got the truck back or not. I just know that it brought my 700 score all the way down to 450. Ouch. Yep, hell hath no fury like a woman scorned.

I didn't give up, though. I did get a 1999 Mazda 2500 pickup truck with a payment of $249.99 a month plus the two cars and a one-thousand-dollar down payment with forty-seven thousand miles on it. With the help of a co-signer whose credit I personally helped build up by using their credit cards and then paying them off quickly. Shot her credit all the way up to an 825. It was also paving the way for her to live a better quality of life. That was the intention, anyway.

Little did I know, she was using other credit cards she had and didn't tell me they were almost maxed out. I could have stopped all of what was about to happen if she had told me sooner. The hurricane was about to hit. She had only been paying the minimum due payment. The cards she was using apparently had very high-interest rates, which in time would destroy her perfect credit. Her income was only about $900.00 a month, while mine was around $3,500.00 then.

I respectfully asked her to cut up those cards and keep the balance on the other cards low, which would have saved her credit. She refused and continued to use the cards, which eventually ended up killing her credit. This would also affect me since my oldest brother's wife messed up my credit to begin with, which took me years to fix. And then the icing on the cake, my ex, surrendering the 1994 Nissan pickup truck because she was royally pissed off at me, which really messed me and my credit up.

The reason why I'm sharing this with you is this: it's vital that you understand the challenges I endured when most people would have just given up because they get too easily overwhelmed by it all. Plus, it would probably drive them crazy. However, that's not the main reason why I'm sharing this with you. The main reason is this: as men, we're supposed to be strong and virile, knowledgeable about certain important things.

Unfortunately, in today's society, most young men don't have a clue about how to act like a man or even what it takes to be a man or what it even means to be a man. In society today, men are being shamed and ridiculed for being and acting like men. Really, what the hell is going on down here on planet Earth? If your intentions are to weaken a society, this is exactly how it's done.

If, however, your intentions are to strengthen a society, you give the men back their personal power by letting them be real men. A real man is a man who protects, honors, respects, and shows compassion to those deserving of it. He will also put them in check if ever needed. A real man will always fight for what's right. He will always stand and fight for a worthy cause, even if it means laying down his life, fighting to protect those he loves.

In today's society, we have young confused boys wanting to wear dresses, bikinis, and walk around in high heels. How is this normal in any way, shape, or form? And why is it becoming considered the new normal in our society today? Who created this movement, and why did they do it? More than likely, these are questions that we'll all have answers to sometime in the future. Eventually, the truth will come to light. The question is when.

I have a simple answer to this very question: it will happen when the men come to the realization that physically, they were always meant to be the strongest of the two sexes, men and women. And recognize that the women need to be wanted. And men, in order to be men, need to be needed. However, I will say this, even though women are emotionally charged human beings, it's through their emotional and mental state that they're the stronger of the two sexes.

Now, for all the women out there who are reading this, this isn't meant or intended as a verbal or emotional attack against you in any way, shape, or form. I respect women who give back and contribute to society and their loved ones. It's the professional victims that I don't respect, who purposefully create and orchestrate the "I'm a victim" facade by declaring they're entitled to certain rights and privileges that others are not entitled to.

Simply because they have no self-respect for themselves or their fellow man. The time has come to set the record straight. We must peacefully challenge these selfish, self-serving, emotionally messed-up individuals by teaching only love the way Our Creator intended for it to be. If society continues on its self-righteous, emotional high horse of entitlement attitude, there will be nothing left for any of us. This includes the following: self-worth, respect, self-respect, and finding our purpose in life.

We are all here on this earth to learn! Along the way through our physical lives, we're going to make mistakes. Isn't that the reason we're all here? I used to train with my sensei three times a week. For those of you who didn't know it, sensei is another word for teacher! He was a damn good sensei at that. He taught me about pressure points, taught me not to resist my opponents, and to be like water, always moving. Bruce Lee knew exactly what he was talking about.

My sensei learned and trained hard to perfect his martial arts skill based on those exact principles. It was my sensei and a palladium knight who pulled me from my pit of darkness that I was sinking into in the early part of 2009. My two good friends, Roddy and Tom, gave Will my number. He taught me swordplay and introduced me to sensei, who was teaching Qigong classes at Cortez Park in Phoenix. Which Will talked me into joining a few months later. Apparently, Roddy and Tom noticed the toll that taking care of my aging mother was beginning to show—all the stress I was going through was becoming obvious every day, as to what this act of love was doing to my emotional and mental state of mind, as well as my overall health and well-being. I needed help. My mother would sometimes drive off in her 1996 Buick, which a neighbor would steal from us. It was parked right in front of our house.

I was beginning to see all of our fake friends starting to crawl out of the woodwork. In packs, just like hyenas do before they're ready to attack. All of a sudden, we had friends who hadn't been there for my mother or me in years, snooping around just to see what they could take as if they hadn't already taken enough back in 2005 when they threw me to the streets by talking my mother into getting an order of protection against me.

They later refused to acknowledge that the attached written statements were their written statements. Oh, and by the way, they were all Black, African Americans, who we thought we knew, whom we considered family throughout the years. The next year, 2006, I would receive a call from Nora with a sense of urgency in her voice, even after all the crap she and her family had put me through.

They demanded that I come home immediately and take care of my mother. Really, who the hell do these people think they are? I was homeless for nine and a half months thanks to their selfish, self-serving, arrogant pride. I was also mugged and robbed at gunpoint after I fell asleep in my teal green Mazda pickup truck. If memory serves me correctly, this all happened around August of 2005, around 9:30 PM.

After being hit in the head twice with the butt of the gun and then repeatedly with the jack handle that the other two were using for their physical assault on me, they wanted my truck. They proceeded to hit me on both sides of my head. It played out like a movie plot gone completely wrong. The first guy hit me twice on my left side. The second guy hit me three times on my right side.

By the way, and this is not being racist, the two men were very small Hispanic men, as was the gunman, who were more than likely here illegally. At first, the one with the gun claimed to be a security guard. Sorry, but security guards don't shine a mini mag-light in your face while pointing a gun directly at you. Now, I already know some of you are probably going to be offended by this statement, and that's okay.

However, in order to truly understand what I'm saying here, go back and read it three or four times. If you choose to do so, I believe you'll come to understand why I included this in the equation. After the assault took place, I ended up with a mild concussion, a torn left ear which required six stitches, and a hole in the right side of my head which required eleven stitches, just above my right temple.

At first, when I blacked out, I thought I was dying, until I woke up and got back on my feet, which was a major task for me, considering the ground appeared to be moving, even though it wasn't. Not to mention, I lost my glasses after the first blow to my right side of the head. After that first blow, all three of them started saying, "Gringo, go down." By the way, in case you didn't know it, "gringo" can be considered offensive depending on how, when, and where it's used. Think about it! Now, where were we?

I ended up driving to the *Seven Eleven* on 59th Avenue and McDowell Road from the incident that took place about two blocks behind the Home Depot location off of McDowell Road. When I got out of my truck and walked in with the jack handle, which was covered in blood—my blood—the sales clerk who was running the cash register apparently thought I was there to rob the store.

Because I was holding the bloodied jack handle in my right hand. Until I explained to him in a slurred voice, due to the fact I was suffering from a mild concussion, that I was the assault victim and needed to get to the hospital emergency room right away, his fear of me and my blood-drenched right side of the face immediately changed to empathy. He even offered me anything I wanted in the store to eat. A faint, painful smile of gratitude emerged from my now very swollen head.

As I was starting to fall down, I reached for the counter to break my fall. As this was happening, the cashier was calling the paramedics for help. When they finally arrived, I was still physically disoriented due to my concussion. And to make matters worse, I was questioned by Bobby Ince, who graduated from the same alma mater, Agua Fria High School, back in 1981.

He apparently recognized me after all those years, even with my bloody face and bloodied clothes. Even though I was in a concussive state, he asked me what drugs I had taken. Apparently, somewhere in his training, he must have forgotten that a concussion can often cause dilation of the pupils.

Which pissed me off! Even though it was obvious that I was still physically incoherent, we made some eye contact. I looked directly at him and said, "You know who you're talking to, right?"

He said yes, then said my name. "Then you should already know the answer to that question."

Bobby then said, "That was a long time ago. People change."

I think he thought since I was obviously homeless at the time that I had turned into a homeless, hopeless drug addict. Looks can sometimes be deceiving. We often see what we believe to be true. We are guilty by association. You see, Bobby was passing judgment on me without knowing the entire story. I believe that maybe he wanted to ask me what the hell happened. He just didn't know exactly how to say it. We often judge others because we're human. It's unfortunate that this often happens.

However, our society, our nation, cannot continue to just give our money away to rehab centers and charitable organizations if they're going to continue the façade of helping people who really don't want to be helped. Think about it like this: if someone truly wants to be better, get better, what should they do? Answer: they repent! The definition of repent is a simple one. It means to change your mind, to no longer do the destructive, addictive things you are doing.

This can lead you into a more productive and fruitful life. You will actually start to like yourself. How do I know? Because it happened to me in the early nineties in Dallas, Texas. I was headed on a self-destructive path, then some very good friends of mine intervened and got me the help I needed to calm my frightened little child inside me. God knew exactly how to get my attention, and my good friend Tom and his wife, the owners of Stampede Country and Western Club, were the willing conduit he used to do it. I thank God for Tom and his wife, and for Lonnie Teague. Without those three in my life when I needed help the most, I probably wouldn't be here to write this book right now. I'm sharing this part of my life with those who need to know they're not alone. But most of all, I'm sharing it with those young men out there who are in their early to late twenties, who feel lost and confused, with no sense of direction, not knowing who to trust.

I've been where you're at right now. It's no fun to go through any of these trials and tribulations. Believe me, I get it. Boy, do I get it! The good news is this: it's part of becoming a man. That which doesn't break can make you. Never ever give up. Always stand tall and strong; that's what a man does. A man also learns to eventually control his emotions. For if a man is in control of his emotions, that man can accomplish anything.

One more thing, men: women love a man who's in control of his emotions. Because they know from our actions if we'll be able to protect them, provide for them, appreciate and love them, and listen to them. Just some very wise and friendly advice, guys. Believe me when I tell you this: you never ever want a woman to become your adversary. There's a reason why they say hell hath no fury like a woman scorned.

Believe it or not, we men, often times like it or not, have to put on our invisible cape and become their hero. In all honesty, it takes a toll on our male egos. But deep down inside, from my experience, it is exactly what every woman wants in a man. What a man should expect in return depends on his actions, reactions, character, and true intentions. Trust me when I say this: they intuitively know within the first week of dating if you're man enough for them.

Even though you may pass this test, there will be more tests coming as the relationship progresses. All you have to do is show them that they can have security in a relationship with you. They want to know they're protected, loved, and respected. However, as a man, you won't just give her respect; she also has to earn it. If she doesn't, she'll never respect you.

And the relationship is doomed to fail. Remember, they want you to be their hero. Being a hero, you're going to pay a very high, illogical, and emotionally charged price. Remember, everything in life starts out with birth pains. We men must decide if the price is too high. Is it worth it? Are they worth it?

Now, this doesn't mean that you become a doormat for her to walk all over! No woman will ever respect you if you let her do this. In her mind, you just became a chump. And women do have a very long memory when it comes to situations like this.

Chapter 9
Reigniting the Fire
Rediscovering Your Purpose and Meaning: Overcoming Burnout and Igniting Your Passion

I have come to realize throughout the years that time waits for no one. It's no secret we're all getting older year after year. We've all done it, fantasized about that one certain fairytale relationship where we're rescuing our beautiful damsel in distress. It's this kind of fantasy thinking that tends to cause what I call the pedestal effect.

If you're not familiar with the pedestal effect, you soon will be. This effect is really hard to recognize at first. It can even take years to realize that you're guilty of doing it. Unfortunately, I am well aware of its symptoms. It will emotionally beat you and tear you down, rob you of your ambitions, goals, and achievements simply because you consciously decided that nothing is more important than pleasing your mate.

Stop. This isn't going to make your life or hers any better. You're two people who are addicted to feelings. Now don't get me wrong here, I'm not saying that you should become a heartless jackass. I'm simply saying to wake up and smell the coffee. Appreciate one another for who you are, take the good with the bad, there's no such thing as a perfect relationship. It takes listening, patience, understanding, and negotiating to make it work.

If a man and a woman decide to fall in love, they both need to stay grounded. Believe it or not, that will ignite not only the fires of passion, it will ignite your desires to go after your goals and achieve greatness. With a mutual level of respect and love for one another, encouraging one another to strive for greatness in everything they do. Because that's what a true life partner does.

There's an old saying: behind every successful man, there's a great woman who he's probably married to, who emotionally supported him even when times were bad, who encouraged him to be great. When I first met Tamara, she put me on a pedestal. The funny thing about pedestals is you eventually fall off of them. What I'm saying here should be easy to understand. Tamara looked at me with the intention of molding me into what she wanted me to be.

And like a fool, I bought into it. In the end, because I did this, she lost respect for me. I, in turn, also lost respect for her. If I had just put my foot down when the relationship started, she would have continued to have respect for me and my goals, ambitions, and achievements. If she and I weren't so busy putting one another on that damn pedestal all the time, our relationship might have been able to survive in the long run.

It would take me two years after we broke up to recover. My zest for life was returning, I had my ambition and drive back. I was starting to feel and see my passion and desire for success reignited. Nothing was going to stop me now; my energy was shifting in the right direction again. When I took my mom to visit her sister in Peoria, Arizona, we stopped at a *Fry's* grocery store off Grand Avenue. I left her side for a few minutes, and this complete stranger, an older woman, said to my mother that I looked like a movie star. These incidents where people were coming into my life confirmed what I already knew. In my subconscious mind, where I secretly planted that seed of seeing the end result as it had already happened.

This would eventually lead me to meeting Ben Johnson, Melissa Gilbert, Harold Sylvester, Jack Palance, Michael Clarke Duncan, Gary Goetzman, Leah Adler (Stephen Spielberg's mother), Don Gerler, Cuba Gooding Jr., Cuba Gooding Sr., Dick Michaels, Ann Richards (the former Governor of Texas who was trying to get me interested in politics), who my former business partners introduced me to. These and many more people like them started to come into my inner circle as soon as I became proactive.

I employed the seven habits of highly effective people. I was attracting these people and more like them into my life because I became so motivated and proactive that they were being drawn to me and ultimately to my true purpose, which was at that point in time to become a leading man, a star in the film industry.

I had come back to life, resurrected from my own personal hell which I unknowingly created. I felt like I was being reborn. This allowed me to point out and deal with, and accept, the mistakes I made throughout my life. Except they weren't really mistakes at all! They were learned lessons, a blueprint of exactly what I needed to improve on in my life to change the status quo.

I started my day with prayer and appreciation for the people and things I had in my life. No matter how big or small they may have been, I was truly grateful for having them. I started to see people differently. I was actually finding the positive in any negative situation I encountered. Thank you again, Adam Roarke (my mentor and good friend), for instilling that into my conscious and subconscious mind.

It has served me well ever since you pointed it out to me that everything and every day is really just a learning experience. If a man doesn't learn from his mistakes, he is doomed to repeat them over and over again. Trust me when I say this: you don't want to be that guy. Men who don't learn from their mistakes often become drifters. Drifters never learn from their mistakes. They often become professional victims.

Victims who'll continue to blame others for their emotional pain and financial suffering. Remember that misery likes company. If this is where you're at right now in life, it's time to flip the switch. It's time to find the positive in the negative. You must be proactive in order to ignite your passion and purpose. Nobody's ever gotten anywhere in life sitting in front of the TV all day, watching television shows from dusk till dawn.

If that's you, stop it now. You were meant to do greater things than these. Don't let a television program dictate to you that your purpose is to just sit and watch TV all day and drink carbonated beverages, and eat comfort foods while you're doing it. Is this really the life that you would want to be your legacy when you die? Of course, it isn't; you'd have to be insane to want to do this day in and day out.

Is it not true that God's one and only begotten Son said to his disciples that they would do greater works than these? According to the Bible, he said exactly that. So, the facts, figures, and witnesses throughout history speak for themselves. How do I know this to be true? It's simple: take a walk around your city or hometown. Look at all the businesses, people driving their cars, the traffic lights, the roads, the freeways, the handheld devices we call cell phones, etc., etc.

What the mind can conceive, it can achieve. In other words, have faith that you will achieve it, then, so be it. For God lives in all of us, and when we truly listen to his voice of wisdom, there are no limits. We limit ourselves based on our belief system. There are three very important principles that must come into play here: mental, physical, spiritual.

If you have all three, nothing is going to stop you from succeeding in anything you do in life. When you have powerful characteristic traits, you become an unstoppable force. Doors (opportunities) that were once closed to you unexpectedly start opening up. As your inner circle continues to grow, you begin to realize that you're more than just a person working a full-time job for minimal pay. You're waking up to the fact that you are an extraordinary human being, who's capable of anything.

Your life now is starting to have new meaning. Congratulations, you've just found your purpose, your reason for being. You start to feel so alive and very aware for the first time in your life. You've become spiritually awakened and mentally aware of everything and everyone around you. Don't believe me? Test it out! Find a quiet place to sit down yoga style, take those earbuds out of your ears, put your phone on silent mode, take a few deep concentrated breaths, breathe in the positive energy, and exhale the negative energy.

I have come to realize throughout the years that time waits for no one. It's no secret we're all getting older year after year. We've all done it, fantasized about that one certain fairytale relationship where we're rescuing our beautiful damsel in distress. It's this kind of fantasy thinking that tends to cause what I call the pedestal effect.

If you're not familiar with the pedestal effect, you soon will be. This effect is really hard to recognize at first. It can even take years to realize that you're guilty of doing it. Unfortunately, I am well aware of its symptoms. It will emotionally beat you and tear you down, robbing you of your ambitions, goals, and achievements simply because you consciously decided that nothing is more important than pleasing your mate.

After doing this every morning for fifteen minutes a day, within about a week you should start to become very aware of all your surroundings, which will enable you to spot future opportunities. How do I know this to be true? It's a scientific fact that our mind, body, and spirit respond and react to frequencies. Everything is a creation of frequencies. If we're going to change our lives and reignite our passion and purpose, we have to change the frequency (attitude is a form of a frequency). Think about it.

If bad habits create more bad habits, which cause a person's character to change, wouldn't it be safe to say that's a frequency? I think it would. Let me explain. We're born, we're taught, we learn a patterned behavior, we develop our character as we mature, we get a job, get married, we can live on this planet for a hundred years or more in good health, depending on our learned program. Get the picture?

Now here's something that's really going to blow your mind. When Yeshua said "Repent, for the Kingdom of God is at hand," what do you think was the real message He was sending when He used the word "repent?" I know what you're thinking: who am I to interpret what His message was or for that matter even speak for Him? Here's what I believe He was saying in four words: to change one's mind. If you really stop to think about it, isn't that exactly what it means? Therefore, by changing your mind, you've successfully flipped the switch and changed the frequency.

Everything and everyone around you is vibrating at a certain frequency. It's all part of our building roadblocks, strains of life known as DNA. Our emotions, our feelings, our beliefs, our character define who and what we'll become. And yes, it's true: as a man thinks it, speaks it, so shall it be. For our tongues have the power to heal, curse, and kill because of the frequencies we either think or speak into existence.

When I officially left Los Angeles, California, to come back to Avondale, Arizona, to take care of my mother, I knew instinctively that I was stepping back into a very low-vibration frequency environment. I also sensed I would more than likely be the only sibling who was stepping up to the plate to do the right thing. The only reason I was able to set foot in Avondale again was because a small group of very good friends in Dallas, Texas, cared enough about me and my future.

And introduced me to Lonnie Teague, an ex-preacher who actually taught me that we always have a choice and there are no accidents in life. This happened at a very low time in my life. Everything has a cause and effect, a Yin and a Yang, therefore everything is based on frequencies. You see, I thought that by moving to Dallas, Texas and getting a fresh start in an entirely new environment, my life would change for the better. Well, I was obviously wrong. Nothing that I touched or did seemed to be working. In my high school graduation yearbook, somewhere inside of it, there was a very profound and powerful biblical quote by the late great Roy Rogers: "A prophet cannot prosper in his hometown." I knew that all the negativity was eventually going to try to creep back into my life once I moved back there.

Even though I wasn't the same abused kid that grew up there, I would still be susceptible to all the negative comments the neighbors would make about me, mostly behind my back. Remember when I told you misery likes company? Well, that was pretty much Avondale, Arizona, in a nutshell. None of the people I went to school with and grew up with knew the language I was speaking.

Even though I was speaking English, it was apparently too much for them to comprehend exactly what I was actually saying. If they would have just adjusted their frequencies a little bit, they would have received and understood what I was saying. Unfortunately, they didn't do that. Instead, due to their low vibrational frequency, they couldn't either see it or didn't want to see it.

So, in closing, I'll leave you with this thought. If God created the world in six days simply by speaking everything into existence, wouldn't it be safe to say that we could do it too? There's power in our words. Our words can emotionally cut us, heal us, bring us peace, love, and understanding. Even in a den of thieves, this is possible. However, if you decide to stay in the city or hometown you grew up in for the rest of your life, you probably won't be able to generate positive frequencies. Only low-level negative frequencies. Why? Because they know how to punch your emotional buttons. Which goes back to the power of the tongue. I will say this though, and this is for all of the children and teenagers and our young men out there who are connecting to these low-level frequencies. Which has caused a lot of fear to spread in our public schools.

It pretty much says that our society is decaying more and more every day. It's time to stop, listen, think, and learn. Change the vibrational frequency. This will in turn stop the school shootings, the suicides, the entitlement looting. Love conquers all; love is the most powerful frequency in the universe. It will take some time to break these patterns of destructive frequencies.

To see the positive changes in our children and young men and young women's attitudes, we must trust and have faith that it will happen, and it will. There are reasons that our Infinite Creator gave us the ten laws, known as the Ten Commandments. I believe it was done out of love. These laws, these instructions, gave us a direct path to the highest frequency of all: love. For love truly does conquer all. Follow it and watch your world and the world around you change.

We have the power to do this if we truly desire it and ask for it. It won't be easy at first; it's going to be hard, like a mother giving birth to her newborn child. Everything in this life started out in either physical pain, mental and emotional pain before it came to life. A painter paints because he or she has a vision and wants to share it with the rest of the world.

When we turned sixteen, if our parents could afford it, we wanted a car so we'd look cool like our other teenage peers we went to high school with. This caused us emotional pain. It would be these painstaking frequencies that would cause us to feel like and be treated like emotional outcasts. We felt looked down upon because we didn't fit in. Our minds started creating drama that wasn't even real just because of the lack of not having a car. Our teenage peers who had cars also had girlfriends.

We didn't. That was another blow to our male egos. After we graduated from high school, we discovered something else: again, here comes the pain frequency. It wasn't the car that made the man, it was the choices he made (labor pains) that eventually made him a man. If he was a provider with ethics, he was not only a man but a good man. If he was a protector, he was a man. The people out in the world today, posting everything they do on social media (which I call the "look at me" syndrome), in my opinion, aren't men, they're attention-starved individuals acting like children who want their cake and eat it too, which spells out a recipe for disaster. They're not vibrating at the frequency that God intended them to. Instead, they're allowing themselves to get sucked into this emotionally driven virtual matrix.

That acts like it's God when it is not. It dictates to them what's acceptable and what isn't, inevitably making you feel like crap because, indirectly, that's probably what their true intentions are. We're being emotionally experimented on, yet we fail to see it because we feel stuck in this low-level vibrational frequency. As we search for the life raft to come and pick us up, we fail to realize the most important thing that really matters the most: our self-worth, our self-respect.

If we'd just turn our heads a little bit in the right direction, we'd not only see that the opinions of others, good or bad, don't really matter. What matters is how we're living our lives. Are we rising up against injustice for all, not just certain races, but all races? Now here's what we call that "aha moment," where we begin to recognize how truly important these words—"United We Stand, Divided We Fall"—really are, not just to ourselves but to all humanity.

Look, the lesson here is so simple it's as plain as the nose on your face. It's time to change the frequencies that we've either been knowingly fed or unknowingly fed. It's time to teach only love, take the blinders off and finally allow ourselves to see the light. Love thy neighbor as you love yourselves, treat others the way you want to be treated. Be that light frequency of hope.

It ain't over, it's never over, unless you want it to be. Life is full of obstacles, except there are really no obstacles in front of you, only hurdles. And what do you do with a hurdle? You jump over it. There's nothing in this life we can't conquer or get through once we change our minds. And decide enough is enough. It's time to change our mind, repent for God's Kingdom is truly at hand, his Kingdom lives in you.

Our physical bodies are his dwelling place. Therefore, we must remember to honor, love, and respect our parents. And parents must also remember to not be quick to provoke their children to anger, for they will become bitter with anger and hatred of heart. If my parents would have just stopped creating these negative patterns of destructive frequencies, I would have turned out differently.

However, I have come to learn throughout time. These things happened for a reason. There are no accidents in life. We must find the positive in the negative frequency. Maybe that reason is this book. For without these experiences in my life, I probably wouldn't have been able to write it.

Chapter 10
Uniting for Change
Mobilizing Communities for a Common Cause

On November 8th, 2008, these words came out of Barack Hussein Obama's mouth: "Change is coming," which was a continuous part of his campaign speech. What he was speaking into existence was what he believed, not necessarily what the American people and the world believed. It was this desire and passion, with the help of Oprah Winfrey, that made him become the 44th President of the United States of America.

How did he do it? What was his weapon of choice that made him President of the United States of America? Did he use magic or smoke and mirrors to do it? Did he pray to God to do it? Maybe. But that's not all he did. He studied every single recorded video and documented speech that former President John Fitzgerald Kennedy ever made that resulted in Kennedy becoming the 35th President of the United States of America.

He modeled himself after JFK simply because he knew that what worked for JFK 47 years ago was going to be a presidential sure-fired win in the early part of the 21st century. How do I know this to be true? It was printed in the Los Angeles Times on March 30th, 2008. When he acknowledged that none of this would ever have happened if not for the generosity of the Kennedy family, they paid for his Kenyan father to travel to America and get an education through Operation Airlift Africa, which was also known as "The Kennedy Airlift."

It's more than obvious, based on the gratitude I'm sure he felt for what the Kennedy family had done for these young Kenyan African students, that Obama chose to use some of JFK's wisdom and words to lock in his running bid for office. He slightly changed the words around and made them his own to get elected. Did he honor America or the Americans who got him the office of President of the United States of America?

That's questionable, something that even today we all still wonder about. Change came alright, but was it really for the good of America and her millions of tax-paying citizens? Before he officially got in office, our country was united. This is the reason we're known as the United States of America. Unity is the key element to any successful and prosperous nation.

When we, the people of the United States of America, stick together and remain united, the political smoke and mirrors tricks stop working. Then our political leaders will be forced into doing the will of the American people and stop playing Russian roulette with our lives and our money. Remember the quote, "A house divided cannot stand." So do our political leaders. President Trump was right; power corrupts when you have it for more than four years as a member of Congress or the Senate.

When everyone comes together for the greater cause, we are more powerful than we realize. United We Stand, Divided We Fall. It is with unity that we become an unstoppable force for the greater good of all. With division, we crash and burn; we fall short of our goals and the right sense of direction on which way to go. Now let's jump ahead eight years after Barack Hussein Obama became president.

It's now November 8th, 2016. The time was around 7:30 PM PST. The winner of the Presidential election was officially announced. Donald J. Trump was officially going to be the 45th President of the United States of America. How did he do it? What former presidential method did he use to win the race to the White House? Was it Abraham Lincoln's? No! George Washington's? No! Richard Nixon's? No! It was former President Ronald Reagan's.

You see, Trump's no dummy. He planned on running for office back in the eighties. If you'd paid attention in the late eighties when Donald Trump appeared as a guest on the Oprah Winfrey Show in 1988, even though he said he had no real intention to run for President of the United States of America, he was dropping subtle hints that he definitely had his eye on getting the job.

Want proof? Here it is! Eleven years later, he went on the Larry King show and discussed the possibility of Oprah Winfrey becoming his Vice President should he actually run. Trump knew that by taking away the possibility of him even running for office, he would win the race to becoming the 45th President of the United States of America simply by making promises using the MAGA campaign (Make America Great Again), almost the exact same campaign slogan Ronald Reagan used, minus the word "Let's."

Now, I'm going to make an educated guess here. Let's assume that Donald J. Trump, even though he wasn't yet President of the United States of America, took notes on everything that Ronald Reagan said during his presidential campaign run back in his 1980 run for office. Or Trump secretly paid someone to do it for him.

A rather shrewd and smart move on Trump's part, which is why I believe he will become the 47th President when the 2024 election is officially over. He may be loud, even a little obnoxious, but he does tend to draw rather huge audiences whenever he speaks. He understands that the United States of America must be run like a business.

In order for America to become great again, unfortunately, under the now-current Biden administration, America is being run like an amusement ride at Disneyland, giving our tax dollars to illegal immigrants who are simply screaming out these words after skipping five or six countries, "Political Asylum!" With no right to it because they haven't even presented any real evidence that they fled their country because their lives were in serious imminent danger.

Why would they allow this unethical act to even happen in the first place? Now look, I know what you're probably thinking right now, that I'm a racist, right? Well, you're wrong in every sense of the word. I'm simply a concerned American taxpayer, just like you, who wants answers. After all, We The People are the real bosses and leaders of the United States of America, aren't we?

So how do we change it? What do we the people need to do to effectively change what's happening to our country? Well, for starters, we all need to back our men and women in blue. By reporting actual crimes in and around our cities, towns, and neighborhoods, we can make a huge difference. An unknown famous philosopher once said this: "The only thing necessary for evil to triumph is for good men to do nothing."

It's time to do something; we can no longer afford to sit idly by and do nothing. How do we do this? By having community get-togethers to discuss these criminal issues and work on finding a solution to successfully take back our neighborhoods and our country. If we don't, we may not have a country anymore.

Now is the time for everyone to become proactive, keep our political leaders in check, enforce our immigration laws, and start arresting these political asylum frauds, and put them in a highly concentrated military prison camp with hard labor for about three months. If we actually did this, I believe our immigration problems would soon be over.

No more free cars, apartments, or money to go to college on the American people's money. Plus, they get $85,000.00 a year for the next three years until their case is heard in a court of law. America has become the world's giving tree, even though we have nothing left to give. We The People must first take care of our own in order to change this financial pitfall America is headed into.

If charity begins at home, then what the hell is going on in our country? We all have an inherent responsibility to ourselves, our families, our children's families, our neighbors, and friends to take action to protect our borders, neighborhoods, land, and homes. It is our God-given right to do so. After all, the Constitution of the United States of America specifically states that We The People have a right to Life, Liberty, and the pursuit of Happiness.

How can any of us live a more productive and fruitful life under these current conditions? With over 250,000 migrant arrests at the beginning of 2024, there's obviously a major The problem that needs to be addressed here is one that requires immediate attention. How can we prosper under these current conditions?

We basically can't. It becomes next to impossible to do so. At this point, the only goal we have left is just staying alive. America is getting dangerously close to the possibility of becoming a third-world country. We can't just sit idly by and allow this to happen. If America falls, everything falls. There will be no more safe places to run to. If we allow this to continue, the only thing left will be survival.

So, how do we stop this from happening? We bring back accountability. We stop screaming "You're a racist" based on the color of our skin and go back to looking at a person's character. After all, wasn't that Dr. Martin Luther King Jr.'s dream that one day his children wouldn't be judged by the color of their skin, but by the content of their character? According to history, it was and still is!

So here's what we need to do: we need to kick political correctness right in the ass and kiss it goodbye (no pun intended). We need to get involved with our communities to restore peace in our cities, hometowns, and neighborhoods. We put down our electronic devices, known as cell phones, and actually start talking to one another again, putting our fears to rest once and for all.

How do we put our fears to rest? By convincing our political leaders that they work for us, not the other way around. It's time to take our country back the right way. It's time to become the United States of America again and remain united. For united we stand, divided we fall. Our duty to ourselves doesn't stop here though; we need to get back to taking care of our health and get our bodies in top physical shape.

A healthy body makes for a strong, healthy mind. When we work out, I mean really work out, it pumps up our endorphins. In doing so, we start to have more energy and feel good about ourselves. We're happier, more productive human beings, living life to our fullest potential. We exist, but we're no longer just existing. Instead of just being alive and existing, we are finding our purpose, our reason for living.

After all, we are all here for a reason, aren't we? So here's a friendly tip if you don't yet understand what I'm talking about. The next time you see an elderly person that might need help getting across the street, ask them if they need any help. If they say yes, take their hand and walk them to the other side. Believe it or not, every older person who's fifty and up has a story to share. That's also an opportunity for the one walking with them to learn something valuable for the future.

For knowledge (information) is power. If it dies, you'll have no more power, and no more personal power means governments can justify stepping in to govern our lives. Didn't President Barack Hussein Obama once make the statement that simple-minded men and women are "too small-minded to govern themselves," and did he not also insist that "order and progress can only come when individuals surrender their rights (their reason for being) to an all-powerful sovereign?"

What was he thinking? Was he even thinking? This isn't England. "We The People" don't submit our will to the crown, do we? I sure as hell hope we don't. But what if this is true? What if that was the plan for America all along? What if everything around us is just some kind of propped-up illusion that tricked us all into believing we're free? And if it is, how do we break free from the governmental chains that bind us all?

Is there really a way out of this *Alice in Wonderland* matrix that was created to enslave every man, woman, and child into submitting to an all-powerful earthly sovereign, if there is such a thing? I believe there is. We simply say no. We don't want this anymore. We want our rights to choose for ourselves what is right and what is wrong, or if you don't like those words, what works and what doesn't.

Our country has one of the highest suicide rates in the world. Based on national statistics, America has the highest suicide rate among middle-aged men and women. Then we have the overly stressed-out 10-hours-a-day or more hourly workers.

We can thank our 43rd President, George Walker Bush, for the extended workday and the hamster wheel effect he created. We basically get up, go to work, then go home to shower and get ready for bed, only to wake up and do it all over again, with only one or two days off a week. Usually, they'll spend those days recuperating their bodies and minds by sleeping in or, in some circumstances, sleeping all day.

All work and no play is a recipe for disaster due to depression setting in. Older baby boomer employees are doing 75 to 80 percent of the work. I know this is true; I've done the research. I've even interviewed older baby boomers who experience these selfish and atrocious acts daily.

Meanwhile, the millennials and generation Xers are getting high in the parking lot on their breaks and lunches, which is illegal. They come back to work high as a kite and hide out, which creates accidents and endangers other people. Most of them are leaving the bulk of the work for the older, more responsible employees. The majority of them are lazy (though there are a few exceptions; I've personally met and worked with them). They're always listening to music through their earbuds and constantly getting on their phones and messing up their pick orders.

This also affects the ones loading the trucks. The corporations, LLCs, Directors of Operations, warehouse managers, supervisors, and leads don't even acknowledge this is happening. They're only interested in getting a paycheck. This is also resulting in more and more violence in and around the workplace. With no real spiritual, emotional, or physical outlets, they either turn to drugs or alcohol for a temporary fix.

Our young men, young women, teenagers, and children become addicted to this process simply because they have no one to freely talk to whom they feel they can trust to share their problems with. That's why there's violence in our schools, workplaces, out in general public, and in our personal and sometimes business relationships as well. Let's face it: we live in a very stressful world, and unless we work together to end a lot of this meaningless stress now, it's not going to get better anytime soon.

The good news is there's always hope. But here's an even better word: "FAITH." Doesn't it say in the Bible that faith is the assurance of things hoped for, the conviction of things not seen? For if we see it, we can change it. Do you see what I see? We learn from doing for others, not just ourselves.

Don't believe me? You soon will. Everything and everyone around you is basically there to be of service to others in some way. Here are a few examples: You go to the grocery store; someone had to put products on the shelves before the store opened for business. You fall in love, get married, and have children. You're now the head of the house, taking care of those you love the most. You're being of service to your family.

Being of service to one another brings us all closer together. Yet, how can a society that's constantly running towards social media for approval of what's right and wrong grow into a more organized, compassionate, and caring society? It can't. Look, I'm not saying that you should cut out social media altogether. What I am saying is don't let it rule you. Instead, you rule it. Humanity is losing its true purpose of being of service to others. We have to become a collective consciousness in order to keep the wolves at bay.

Staying home, playing nothing but video games every day, sitting around binge-watching movies, smoking a blunt or a joint, isn't going to make our problems go away. We must confront our fears head-on, using a rational mind to do so. This opens up and broadens our minds to one another, causing an endless wave of unity for the greater good of humanity. This, in turn, gives us all a purpose and a reason to want to live.

So get out there, get involved in your communities, and make a difference. You have a voice; we all have a voice. Use your voice, not violence, to change the status quo. Now is the time for all men and women to come to the aid of their country. Unity is power; there's real strength in numbers.

Chapter 11
A World Transformed
The Ripple Effects of Collective Actions Inspiring Change on a Global Scale

We're all unique in some way, shape, or form. It's through our uniqueness and our ability to see things that others can't, that makes us all unique. We all have the frequency in us to change our lives, our relationships, and even the world. To transform it into becoming a better and more civilized place. No, I'm not talking about the new world order. I'm talking about humanity coming together for the greater good of all. Unity is the most powerful and logical way to keep our governments honest.

Every single human being on the planet has a voice. It's the responsibility of each and every one of us on the planet to use our voices wisely and responsibly. We as a society must not allow the overly emotionally charged, uneducated younger generation to continue on this self-destructive course.

They need guidance (a mentor) to teach them about common sense, discipline, and character. These are the very essential elements and ingredients needed for success in their chosen fields of profession, as well as their personal and business relationships. This will not be an overnight process. It's kind of like getting ready to bake a cake, but if you leave out one of the most essential (important) ingredients, the cake is going to fall.

Everything in life takes time. Establishing ourselves and finding out where exactly we fit into society takes time. Starting a family takes time. Starting a new career takes time. Raising your children takes time. Time, what exactly is time? Believe it or not, time is the most valuable asset we all have on this planet. Once we have this figured out, we not only develop an appreciation and respect for it, we actually start to value it more and more each and every day of our lives.

If respect isn't just given, which by the way it isn't, it's earned. Then shouldn't we show more respect for time in order to earn its respect? You better believe we should. Think of it like this: you're out in the Superstition Mountains in Arizona exploring. Suddenly and unexpectedly you stumble upon the greatest discovery of all time—the Lost Dutchman Mine. So now what do you do? Do you call the legal authorities and tell them about your discovery? More than likely you wouldn't, but you probably should!

So now it's starting to get a little more complicated. Your mind starts racing as your adrenaline levels start to increase, your heart races as the excitement builds up. Now you're facing the fight or flight syndrome. A few seconds, maybe five to ten seconds, have passed since the incident. I'm sure that you probably get the picture now; time is a valuable thing.

During the fight or flight phase, it's next to impossible to grasp how much time has passed from when the incident started to when it ended. This is only natural as it's in all of our DNA. It protects us from potentially dangerous situations and can prevent us from making the wrong choices when we pay attention to it! This can even go for doing what's right versus doing what's wrong. In other words, it's like a built-in subconscious warning that slaps us in the face to get our attention, which in turn leads to the fight or flight response.

Usually, you only have seconds to make the right decision to run or stay.

You might be thinking at this point, what does any of this have to do with a global transformation? And how is it relevant to a worldwide transformation for the good of mankind? It has everything to do with who we want to be, who we want to become, and are we willing to pay the price and confront our very fears that paralyze us from proceeding on to achieving greatness and transforming our world into a more fruitfully productive producing machine, which will in turn continue to bear fruit for many generations to come.

Once we get past our fears, the sky's the limit. Didn't Jesus, according to the Bible, tell his disciples that they would do greater works than these when he was doing the works of his Father in Heaven on earth? Was he talking about miracles or mankind's capability of achieving greatness simply by believing it already happened? What the mind can conceive, it can achieve. Is it possible that this was exactly what Jesus indirectly was really trying to teach them?

Anything is possible if we believe it is! However, in today's world, most have fallen prey to socialism, big brother, aka government, and technology crutches.

Their spiritual antenna with their Creator has been broken for a long time. The reception is no longer clear! Their spiritual frequencies are not aligned with their Divine Creator. They're drifting through life with no real sense of direction.

All men, especially men, have to know that they are needed. A man that is not needed is like a fish out of water; if the fish has no water, the fish will die. If a man is no longer needed, his purpose for living becomes obsolete. He feels like nothing matters anymore; an emotional wave of worthlessness hits the very depths of his heart and soul. This has become a serious problem in our country today. Our young men have become emotionally dependent, which isn't normal for any man.

Men, we're meant to be the protector, the provider, the hunter. Men were once revered and respected, but not anymore. What in God's name happened, and why? Believe it or not, it all started with the women's liberation movement from the 1960s to the early to mid-1970s all over the United States of America and later to other parts of the world.

Now, don't get me wrong here, it's not my intention to piss off the female population in the USA, or for that matter, any other country on the planet. It is, however, my intention to get every man and woman's attention. To get both sexes to take a step back, take a deep breath, and examine the world's history. To find a way to fix what went wrong. If our country, the good old USA, continues on this course of self-destruction, and there are no real men left to defend and fight for our country, then all our enemies would have to do at this point is just walk in and take over America. Hopefully, you're starting to see just how badly America needs her men, and young men, to be able to protect our borders and every woman and child who can't defend themselves. See, men are needed after all, so why then are we so undervalued and disrespected? I blame the system for allowing the castration of the American male to happen.

I believe that if those women who screamed and protested for equal rights—which, by the way, includes the following: equal pay, job equality, equal rights, the very same rights that the working men once had—according to demographics, we still do. I don't agree with that equation, though!

Based on what I learned when I had to make a choice to go back to working for Corporate America. So what exactly went wrong here? How did we get to the current destination we're at now? What transformational change caused this domino effect with our American men and the rest of the world's male population? Believe it or not, it was the women's liberation movement.

This movement was gaining some serious momentum back in 1973 when Helen Reddy's album, *I Am Woman* produced by Capitol Records, hit the number one spot on the Billboard Hot 100! It seemed like every woman in America was not only tuning in to hear her number one hit song, "I Am Woman" but they were also buying her records, which caused her album to hit platinum status, meaning it hit one million copies sold.

By the early nineties, her album resurfaced, this time going double platinum as it hit the two million copies sold status. Helen Reddy would go on to produce more successful albums. How do I know this? Because my oldest brother Mark used to love listening to her music. He also liked listening to Burt Bacharach, Neil Diamond, the Beatles, the Rolling Stones, and the Moody Blues. There were others that he listened to as well, but these are the ones I remember.

Now, I'm sure you're probably wondering, what does this all have to do with the overall current events taking place in America and the rest of the world today, right? Good, because here's where it starts to get a little tricky.

According to God's Ten Commandments, which I'm sure we all have broken at some point in our lives, especially this one: Thou shalt not have any other gods before me. Hmm, you're probably wondering why I picked the first Commandment, right?

Well, isn't it obvious that if we all, men and women both, kept any of God's Commandments, especially this one, history just might have played out differently for both sexes? I believe it would have, and here's why: If men and women had stuck to God's covenant (the contract made with God by a man and a woman known as marriage), there would have never been a women's liberation movement. Instead of trusting God's wisdom and better judgment, our married women were running to the courts and hiring greedy lawyers who were only interested in one thing—money. Money they would eventually find once a motion for divorce was filed. Most of the time it was the married woman filing for divorce, attempting to take the man for everything he had. Bottom line, divorce is big business for any lawyer when there's big money involved.

Ok men, you can stop gloating now and listen very carefully to what I have to say here. Or is it possible that God was trying to get the men's attention before the women's liberation movement ever started? Answer: yes, because anything is possible, right? You see, I personally believe that women's lib would never have happened if the women felt that the men valued and respected them.

Unfortunately, in the women's eyes, we didn't. After all, we're the men, right, and what we say goes, right? Nope, that kind of macho man mentality is probably the key reason why the divorce rate in America is the second highest in the world. In the 21st century, men and women are now competing against one another on a daily basis. They're competing for jobs, money, recognition, fame, and fortune. They used to say that for every male there were ten women. Now they're saying that for both sexes, it's about even now. Hmm, I wonder why? What changed that pretty much evened the playing field for both sexes?

The answer is that the persona of living a fairytale romance got smacked right in its face. The women became overwhelmed with all of their work duties, while the men started to slowly disconnect from society. Instead of protecting and providing for their family and loved ones, they started to act like the jilted woman.

They don't even have a clue that they're doing it. They know something isn't right with them; they just can't seem to pin down the source. Houston, we have a problem. Come in, mission control, do you read me? Loud and clear, Houston. Finally, the light bulb turns on, and the answer is starting to materialize. Now the question is, how do we fix it?

We start by acknowledging that our society is broken, our men and young men are broken, and our system is broken. Just like the story of Humpty Dumpty who sat on a wall, had a great fall, and all the king's horses and all the king's men couldn't put Humpty Dumpty back together again. Fortunately for our society, our men, young men, and our system, this does not have to be the case.

If we come together as a collective consciousness, we can fix our broken system, which in turn would fix our broken men and young men, including our society. This would actually fix all of these issues simply by acknowledging what happened was wrong. Look, I know there's always going to be someone out there somewhere who's reading this and saying either in their mind or out loud, "haters gonna hate." Stop it, this isn't hate; this is information to help those who want help. Haters, from what I've observed, are mostly the ones saying it just so they can justify their actions simply because they refuse to grow up. That's it, that's what I see from what I've witnessed throughout the past ten years of my life.

This isn't helping our men, young men, our system, or society to become a stronger and more productive race. What it is doing is transforming humanity into a bunch of cry babies, aka haters, finger-pointing blame game individuals who refuse to accept responsibility for their actions. Instead of owning up to what they've done, like a man would, they start crying "hater" or "my bad."

Whatever happened to saying you're sorry and meaning it? What happened to repentance and owning up to your own mistakes? I believe it actually started in the early to late 90s when the Jerry Springer show was about to get canceled if the producers didn't start to implement some serious changes. When the show first launched, it was basically a political forum talk show with very low ratings.

How do I know this? I witnessed it. The show platform eventually changed in 1994. How do I know this to be true? Because my ex, Tamara Davis, and her daughters posed in the August 1993 Conehead edition of Playboy magazine with Pamela Anderson and Dan Aykroyd on the cover. She came to me and asked me if I would go on the show with her, before the show's format changed, and act like we just met. The producers and Jerry Springer thought it would give their ratings a huge bump. Apparently, it was the age difference between

Tamara and me that got their attention, plus a photo of me that she told me she showed to one of the producers of the show.

I almost agreed until Tamara told me how it was going to play out. She wanted me to act like a star-struck puppy love guy that she agreed to meet with on the Jerry Springer show because my love-crazed letters apparently got her attention, and she was excited to meet me, but only on the Jerry Springer show. It was a publicity stunt to make her look good, but it was much worse than a publicity stunt; it was a lie that would have haunted me and my career interests for the rest of my life. Believe it or not, I think she got the idea from Cher's ex, whom Tamara actually met on another talk show they were both on.

Needless to say, I flat out refused to agree to appear on the show based on the false pretenses that were presented to me. Not to mention that in the entertainment industry, once you lie, it comes back to haunt you. I even discussed it with my mentor Adam Roarke. He immediately said, "Don't do it, you'll never go anywhere in the entertainment industry if you do. That lie will haunt you for the rest of your life."

I shook his hand, thanked him for telling me what I already knew, then went back and delivered a heartfelt thank you, but no thank you. Tamara was pissed. She couldn't believe I actually said no. About two months later, the Jerry Springer show officially changed gears, their ratings started going through the roof, and America and her values started going down the toilet.

The evidence speaks for itself: our country had fallen under the Jerry Springer show spell! Our morals and ethics were starting to slip away. Talk show drama, baby mama drama, swingers and stripper drama, family drama, cheating relationship drama, religious drama, and fist fights on the show drama. What the hell happened to America? The country that was once known as the light of the world was becoming very dim.

Her light was beginning to burn out. Political correctness was growing rapidly in and around America. The younger generation was becoming more and more rebellious and disrespectful towards law enforcement, their parents, and even complete strangers.

They even started having sex and getting pregnant. They were babies having babies and demanding that their parents take care of them and the baby. America was becoming a messed up, codependent nation.

A nation of emotionally mixed-up and messed-up children who would never grow up. The fall of America was officially starting to happen. Just as history predicted after Hiroshima and Nagasaki, a statement was made by a world leader that one day our country would be brought to her knees. But it wouldn't happen on the war front battlefield; it would happen in our schools through our children. There's a reason why they say that children have impressionable minds, for they are easily influenced.

The American government and the American people laughed at what was said. For she was the strongest country on Earth, and nothing or nobody was going to ever be able to take her down. America had developed an overconfident, cocky, arrogant attitude. She had become too sure of herself, and why shouldn't she be? She was the top-producing country on the planet.

There's an old saying that still stands true today: the bigger they are, the harder they fall. It doesn't take a genius to figure out what happened, where and when it happened, and why. It's as plain as the nose on your face. America dropped her guard. She and the American citizens weren't paying close attention to the history of countries that were conquered through socialism and what was currently transpiring in present-day events.

America was too sure of herself, and that would eventually mean that one day she was going to fall. How exactly that would happen was questionable at the time. Three decades later, it was becoming very clear as to the reason for her demise. America had forgotten about God. She became emotionally and spiritually bankrupt after turning her back on God. Apparently, America had forgotten that charity begins at home.

America was actually biting the very hand that had been feeding her for years: the American taxpayers. You're probably thinking, how could we allow this to happen, right? I have an answer, but you might not like it! We the people did this to ourselves when we quit praying and talking to God to help us find our way out of the darkness. We the people decided not to keep our government officials in check. We became complacent. We quit exercising, I mean really exercising. We wanted the very best that life has to offer without paying the price.

With the rise in technology, only a few of us could see how badly damaged our country was getting. Unfortunately, this trend hasn't stopped. There are only two ways to stop it: doing God's will and developing a strong moral character. I find it interesting and disheartening that America was once considered a beacon of hope, the light of the world. Not anymore. She's become the milking pot of the world. A very selfish world!

There's a hidden gem of a movie from the 70s known as *Soylent Green* which takes place in New York City. The setting is in the year, hmm, now this is a bit of a coincidence, as the setting takes place in the year 2022. I'll leave that interpretation up to you. *Soylent Green* starts out kind of slow. At first, the movie makes no sense. Basically, it plays out like a very bad detective love story in an age where mankind has completely abandoned God's laws, love, and wisdom to guide them back to a moral and godly character. But, you know as well as I do that in making a movie, you have to have peaks and valleys, ups and downs. Without any of that, you have no story of interest.

Anyway, back to *Soylent Green*. Eventually, after experiencing the good life, eating real food and not *Soylent Green*, with a beautiful ex-girlfriend of a now-dead multi-billionaire, I think he was a billionaire, who was the man who created this dystopian world by preaching religiously about the greenhouse effect.

I find it interesting that eleven years later the movie *1984* which, if my memory serves me correctly, came out in the latter part of 1984. Was this just a coincidence? Or is it possible that even though these were once just movie scripts now made into movies, maybe the writer or writers already knew something about the future and where we were heading? After all, anything's possible, isn't it?

If society doesn't stop doing what it's currently doing—being reckless, leaving most of the work for the Baby Boomers in the workplace, being willfully ignorant, drag racing on public streets, and getting high all the time, drinking liquor and beer excessively, texting and driving, disrespecting others and falsely justifying it—then isn't the next step to enslave us all into submitting our will to an unknown all-sovereign entity?

I think it is! But we can stop this from happening to our country and ourselves if we pull our heads out of our butts and start thinking for ourselves again. We can work towards a brighter future to enrich our lives, our children's lives, and our beloved country, the United States of America. I mean, after all, if a former dictator like Adolf Hitler actually came into power by telling the Jewish people that they were the disease and he was the cure, and they believed it, then think how much more power we actually have by simply telling the truth. Which I believe would change the direction that America is heading in right now. Hitler also said that if you tell a lie and keep on telling it precisely the exact same way, eventually they'll begin to believe it as the truth. Hitler was referring to the Jewish people when he said it.

When you stop and actually think about it, history is repeating itself through our government leaders. Did they sell "We The People" of the United States of America out, just like Hitler did with the Jewish people? It's very possible, and that alone is something that every single American taxpayer should be concerned about. We The People, must call out our political leaders for crossing the socialist line and put them in check for everything they've done.

While they're in office, they're supposed to be representing the American people instead of lining their pockets with the taxpayer's money. Okay, so now what? Where do we start? Or better yet, how do we even start to end these transgressions our political leaders have all more than likely committed against each and every American taxpayer? By keeping us all focused on race issues, immigration, border issues, etc., etc.

Why are we busy fighting one another, which we shouldn't be doing? It's a set-up. Keep us distracted, and our government is free to pass the very laws that will make them wealthy. It's a sleight of hand parlor trick. Every great illusionist knows exactly how to do this without the audience ever suspecting a thing. In our world today, through the internet, we the people are waking up. We're finally starting to realize that maybe, just maybe we've been played for a very long time.

The good news is if this is true, we the people really do have the power to change it. So, how is any of this even relevant to transforming our government, our countries, our world, and our young men and women into a moral and ethical character-filled and respected nation of God-loving, moral, and ethical people? It's simple, really. If power corrupts, and it actually does, unless you have the voice (your conscience) of God directing you, you won't be corrupted. True wisdom, which comes from God, tends to keep us on the straight and narrow. By actually electing true God-loving and fearing, wisdom-filled political leaders who actually honor God's commandments (rules of law), America and her youth will slowly witness their lives and America changing course, steering her and our youth in the right direction. And once again reestablishing herself as the light of the world.

I remember what my grandmother said to me many times when I was younger: "Keep your eye on the ball, and watch your dreams come true. If you don't catch the ball, someone else will." Sounds like this is what happened to the United States of America and the rest of the world, doesn't it? Isn't it time for us all to catch the ball and get back to God and his godly principles? I think it is!

Chapter 12
The Legacy Lives On
Perseverance Through Generations Passing the Torch of Compassion and Heroism

When I was a little boy, I would often fantasize that I was James West, the government secret service hero from the TV show *The Wild Wild West*. Since my oldest brother liked the show, I looked up to him, I actually think I wanted to be him. James West was a real live government agent who worked directly for President Grant with his sidekick Artemis Gordon, affectionately known as Arty by his partner James West.

Our mother and father were always constantly fighting with one another. And our mother would always threaten to leave my father and take us kids with her. With both of them constantly physically and verbally abusing one another on a weekly and sometimes daily basis, this was really starting to mess with our lives.

Apparently, they were both so busy fighting with each other that they couldn't see the lifelong damage they were inflicting on their own children's overall mental well-being. This would stay with us, especially me and my brothers, for the rest of our lives, all the way into our transformation from young boys to becoming full-grown men. I would often crawl under my bed when they (our Mom and Dad) were fighting and pray to God to stop them as the fear of not knowing what to expect was building up inside of me. I lay quietly crying and praying to God to stop them from fighting. Sometimes it worked; sometimes it didn't. Sometimes it got so bad that we (their children) had to step in and break it up. My father always seemed to be the one with the cuts and bruises most of the time when these arguments continued to escalate to a volatile level. My brothers and I would spring into action to break them up.

I would often hear the theme song from the former TV show *The Wild Wild West* playing over and over in my head when these arguments popped back up. I believe in my mind at those very moments of my life that I was James West, working towards establishing peace in my country and government once more. I was the secret service agent, my brothers were the government, and our mom and dad's anger towards one another was the ticking time bomb that I was sent to deactivate and rid the country of this would-be explosive threat.

I even put together my own James West outfit using some old linoleum that I found in the storage room at the apartment we were living in. Kids need heroes, especially kids who were raised in totally dysfunctional families. When a child has someone they can respect and look up to, it gives them hope that a better life is waiting for them in the future.

James West was my hero, even though he was a fictional one created by Hollywood writers. Watching *The Wild Wild West* restored my faith that there were still good people in the world. I think that kids today don't feel like they really have any hope or vision for a brighter future. They're constantly being bombarded with negative influences, thanks to the internet.

They can surf it or download information for just about anything. They appear to be under some kind of hypnotic spell that's consistently feeding them and filling their minds with negative thoughts, feeding them destructive and often character-damaging information due to the lack of real parental guidance, understanding, and love, which they desperately want and need.

They're so full of rage and hate that they eventually just give up. The most accepted way to give up and give in for them, unfortunately, is suicide. This is unacceptable. It's got to stop. They are crying out through social media for help before they're getting ready to commit suicide. Their frightened little child is crying out for help in a self-destructive way. They need a mentor, a hero to take them by the hand and tell them, "My door is always open to you. If you need me, here I am."

That's basically what happened to me when I was growing up. I always had someone somewhere reaching out to help me stay emotionally balanced. I didn't have all these electronic device distractions our youth have today. Plus the fact that I truly believed in the power of prayer at the time, and still do today. For even though I didn't really realize it yet, God was actually answering my prayers through the people that were coming into my life.

It was my epiphany, my awakening so to speak, that golden light bulb moment in time when the picture became incredibly clear. I had not only withstood the test of time to become the man I was meant to be, but I finally understood the real principles I would need to apply to change my life and be of humble service to my community, family, and friends. It is, however, unfortunate that they couldn't or wouldn't see it that way.

Instead, they (my family and those who called themselves my friends) thought I was just looking out for myself. If that was indeed true, then why did I decide to leave more than several very promising opportunities to take care of my mother? That would have changed my life substantially—spiritually, emotionally, and financially! Because of my belief system (morals and ethics), I left my shot at true happiness with a beautiful Scottish woman I really loved and respected.

I gave up a life with Beverly—that was her name—because my mother was having some issues, which sent my intuition antenna straight up, sending me signals that something wasn't right. When food tasted like soap because my mom was hand washing her dishes without rinsing them off, I knew something wasn't right, especially when she would cook for both of us, and the food tasted like soap, which she apparently couldn't taste.

Then a good friend who was like a father to me, Jack Williams, died on May 11, 2008. He had called me in 2007 asking me to move in with him and take care of him. His wife, Helen, had recently passed away. He told me that all the money, cars, and the house would be left to me in his will after he passed away. He also said that he would pay me $500.00 a week to do it.

I politely and respectfully said to him the following: "Jack, I'm sorry, but I'm taking care of my mother now. It just wouldn't be right to leave her by herself alone. She needs me right now." He was desperate; he even begged me to come back to Dallas because he didn't trust anybody but me to help him. I said if things were different, I'd come there in a heartbeat.

Jack Williams, when he died, was worth about $1,500,000.00 in property and assets. That would have been all mine had I gone to Dallas and stayed with him for what would be his last year on Earth. Jack had Parkinson's disease, which he'd been battling since 1992. He lost the fight for his life to Parkinson's on May 11, 2008.

I found out when I tried calling him to check on him in March of 2009. His home phone had been disconnected, which told me something wasn't right. So I called his old business number, 1-800-LABLEMAN. I then asked the current owner of Jack's former business if I could speak to Mitch. At first, she refused. Then, when I told her who I was and about the relationship I had with Jack for years, she finally put Mitch on the phone.

What Mitch shared with me next broke my heart. After I asked if Jack was okay, Mitch was completely silent for what seemed like an eternity. His response was, "You don't know, do you?"

I said, "Know what, Mitch?"

Then he just said it: "Jack passed away about a year ago. I'm sorry, man, I know how much Jack meant to you."

I said, "Thank you, Mitch. I appreciate it. Now I know. Thank you."

The funny thing about all these opportunities that were once there for the taking is that if I only would have said yes, maybe I would have been better equipped at handling the whole situation. And Beverly would have become my wife and the mother of our beautiful children. Unfortunately, my final decisions changed all of that.

Even though I told the nosy neighbor across the street in 2007 about Jack's very generous offer, which I humbly turned down, they somehow managed to turn my words completely around. What's worse is they told my mother that I was going to move back to Dallas, Texas, just so I could inherit Jack's estate. My mother was pissed at me the next day I returned home from working at Atlas, a food warehouse located in Tolleson, Arizona.

Nora, one of our longtime neighbors, had apparently convinced my mother that I was going to be moving back to Texas, which meant pretty much to hell with my mother. This caused me to have a considerably somewhat verbally hostile conversation with my mother based on a very false pretense that the neighbors had planted in her mind. How in the world could anybody screw up very simple English and change the meaning of my words to basically, "Fuck you, I don't care about you. I'm going where the money is?"

This comes from neighbors who said they just wanted to mind their own business. Apparently, that was either a lie, or they have a serious selective memory problem or a possible hidden agenda from the very start. When I made my decision to move back to Arizona in 2001 to help my aging mother, who was obviously showing more signs of her mental decline, what kind of son would I be if I just stayed in L.A., knowing full well what was happening to my mother?

Not a very good one, that's for sure. And nobody else (my siblings) was stepping up to the plate to do it. I was left alone and by myself to pick up the pieces of my mother's life. I was the one who always told her, "One day, I'm going to buy you a big house with a butler to take care of the house and a limousine driver who will take you anywhere you wish to go," which never happened because my mother was always begging me to help my brothers without a thought of what it would do to me and my life in the future.

All she kept saying was this: "Out of all my children, you're the only one who seems to have the natural ability to bounce back and land on your feet again and again." I tried to explain to her it was the self-help books I had been reading throughout the years and continued to read that installed the very knowledge into my conscious and subconscious mind that gave me that ability to tap into my imagination and creative side, which led me to those moments of sink or swim.

Instead of drowning, I chose to swim. As my adrenaline increased, so did my awareness of my surroundings. My conscious mind was yelling at me, telling me it won't work. However, I had a secret weapon. I had learned through all the self-help books I had read how to shut up my conscious mind using my subconscious mind to battle with my conscious mind. It was at that point in time that I was becoming unstoppable. But unfortunately, just like Superman, I had my own kryptonite (women), which I vowed I would stay away from until I made it. The only problem was that, unbeknownst to me, when I made the choice to move back into the house I basically grew up in, I had unwittingly broken my own vow to myself. Even though I wasn't in a sexual relationship with any of these women, it didn't really matter. Once I moved back to my old neighborhood, I slowly began to see that these women, my mother included, were attacking my character based on how the men who were previously in their lives had treated them. In other words, they were all emotionally damaged goods. I just happened to conveniently become their targeted whipping post. Remember when I said misery likes company? It's true; it does.

You see, even though I had officially stopped playing the white knight and quit rescuing or trying to rescue every damsel in distress that came into my life, I still had somehow indirectly set myself up to do it all over again when I made a conscious decision to take care of my mother, with no real thought of what I had done to myself.

Here's the key moral of this story. Now, listen very carefully to these specific words. In order to help others, we must first help ourselves. We can't save those who don't want to be saved. This is probably going to sound kind of vain, but I don't care. It needs to be said, especially to the men and young men out there. Never ever allow those you love—your family, relatives, or friends—to steal your thunder or your happiness, no matter what the stakes are. Isn't it better to fight for your rights and what you believe in than to live a complete lie based on what others believe to be true?

A great man once said something like this: "A human being is a whole being who the Universe calls (God) to experience the illusion of life, matter, space, and time in the physical sense. To experience life in a prison-like state, which we freely chose to create according to a contractual agreement we can't remember signing to experience life on this physical plane."

The man who shared this with me passed away in April of 2016. He was my sensei and good friend who had been sexually, physically, and mentally abused by his father when he was 12 years old. He shared this with me after he forgave his father for everything he'd ever done to him while holding his hand as he took his final breath just before he passed away.

Wow, he was not only a great man, he was a hero. I tried to encourage him before he passed away to tell his story to the world, as it would have helped a lot of people out in the world to heal their mind, body, and soul. That was like nine months before he died. The book never got written. When I was introduced to Ron, my sensei, by William Nelson, who taught me sword play, William was a Paladin Knight. I was tired, emotionally and spiritually beaten, which they noticed by the low energy in my voice and my body language.

They might not have known it at the time, but I was about ready to give up. Remember what I said earlier about God answering my prayers? I didn't know it at the time because I pretty much believed God gave up on me. So I had quit praying and asking for help. Even though I was pissed at God for the way my life had turned out. After crying my butt off in my sister's old bedroom with the door locked and blocked with a chair pushed under the doorknob, hearing my mother yelling and demanding me to open the door, calling me worthless and a few other really explicit names I won't mention here, I will say this though: it put me in complete shock due to my lack of being able to get any real sleep, caused by my mother's cognitive decline. I was ready to toss in the towel. Then I got down on my knees as my mother continued to beat on the door, demanding that I let her in.

I begged God to take me away. He didn't. Instead, I heard these words: "I'm not the one who created these problems that you're experiencing right now."

I replied, "If you're not, then who is God?"

I received a very loving but firm response: "Mankind did this; I didn't. I don't interfere with what mankind does. They have free will. It's their free will, without my guidance and words, that's created these current conditions."

I give to those who knock on the door and ask. You quit asking, so I couldn't step in and take the wheel. Yet now you ask and have your answer. The choice is yours. I was officially, for a time, fully repented. It became very painfully clear that I chose to do this. Nobody had put a gun to my head and demanded I go back to Arizona and help my mother.

It was all becoming very clear to me now. God was and always had been answering my prayers. He did it through the people that he put in my life. Just like the footprints story, He was carrying and guiding me in the right direction all along. I was just too blind because of my pride to see it. It did teach me a very valuable lesson, though: to always be grateful for everything and everybody that's put into your life.

For it's with true gratitude that we learn to appreciate everything that life throws our way. For there is true wisdom we can all inherit from our life's experiences. Just like the lesson where the teacher says to his student, "When you can grab the pebble from out of my hand, it will be time for you to go." In other words, he would hopefully continue his quest in his search for true wisdom.

As he continued to walk barefoot in the desert, seeking the answers to life's questions, "Why are we here?" Eventually, he figured out that this planet, this plane we call Earth, was his school, teaching him the wisdom of the ages to pave the way for a better world for the generations to come. In the end, he had fulfilled his contractual agreement between himself and God.

He had found his purpose in this life. And he definitely made a big difference in other people's lives whose paths he crossed. He wasn't just a martial arts teacher. He held a doctorate in Chinese medicine, was a former Naval officer, a father, a friend, an advisor, and a part-time talent promoter who went by G-Balls when he was promoting his grandson's rapping talents.

The name G-Balls got him a lot of attention. I think that's why he picked it. He knew it was going to get the phone ringing, and it actually did. I think that's why he asked me back in 2010 to take over his style of martial arts (Fujikai). Yep, just like Bruce Lee, Ron had created and invented his own martial arts style and wanted his legacy to live on through me. I probably would have accepted if I didn't have to take care of my mother.

This would have definitely been a back door for me to use to get back into the entertainment industry as an action hero and martial arts actor and have my own style of martial arts to teach and practice, which would have definitely worked to my overall advantage. Again, I instinctively knew that with everything on my plate, my plate was already full. I respectfully thanked him for thinking of me, then turned him down. I could see the confusion and disappointment dancing around in his eyes.

You see, I really wanted to do it. But I had other responsibilities I needed to take care of first, which I knew were going to take some time to get everything done. Nobody was going to do it for me, that's for sure. I had to be the hero in this whole equation. My brothers, my sister, my relatives, and the people who called themselves my friends obviously had no interest in stepping up to the plate and lending a helping hand.

It's often stated that the middle child or the oldest child will be the one who will take care of their aging parents or parent when they're no longer able to fend for themselves. Because they can't remember how to get to the grocery store or where their car keys are, they're constantly falling down and getting bruised up. Or worse, they break some bones, which usually never heal one hundred percent. They get easily frustrated as they're starting to realize they're losing their independence and can no longer afford the luxury of living alone.

They realize their quality of life is changing. They feel totally lost and scared. Life has dealt them an unfair hand. Unfortunately, no one ever said life was fair. As they seek out a life raft to grab onto (one of their children), it's usually the middle or oldest child, who is now grown into a full-grown man or woman, that they're looking to save and protect them from the unknown world they subconsciously know they're slipping into.

That son or daughter, whether they know it or not, just became, at that very moment, their parent's or parents' caregiver and guardian. They now have apparently become their parent's or parents' hero. It is said that we come into this world with nothing and we will leave this world with nothing. The only thing we really have left is our memories (our legacy) of the life we lived. Isn't it time we all take a step back and examine our lives?

In doing so, we will not only become aware of all our transgressions, but we will be spiritually awakened by the overall experience and become enlightened beings. What exactly is enlightenment? In my opinion, it's a knowing, an understanding that defines one's life purpose. I've come to a realization ever since I chose to leave a very toxic relationship years ago with my ex, Tamara Davis.

God rest her soul! Tamara died on the evening of December 29, 2021, from COVID-19. Even though we were no longer together, I still loved her unconditionally and wished her well always. I even prayed for her for a season. I was grateful for her coming into my life. She brought me out of my shell. Before we met, I was a man of few words. Being with her changed all of that. Meeting and being with her was both a blessing and a curse, of which I don't regret.

Everything happens for reasons we don't yet under-stand. It's when we take a few steps back that we begin to see what's on our horizon. When I met Tamara, she was so full of life. She respected me, and I respected and protected her. In the beginning, I was her knight in shining armor. She always joked about me rescuing her from her captors that were holding her in a high tower, waiting for me (her knight) to rescue her (my damsel in distress) to take her away to a new life together. We were like two giddy school kids at first. Then something changed. Our relationship was heading into stormy waters. Apparently, she either forgot I was younger (15 years) than she was. Her patience had started to wear thin. Our once fairytale relationship was slowly falling apart. I still loved her, though, even though we hit our point of no return. I just wasn't in love with her anymore.

Even though this is about the beginning, middle, and end of mine and Tamara's relationship, it's a vital part of the last chapter of my book. Because knowing her, being with her, and experiencing life with her for almost 10 years made me become the man I am today, of which I have very few, if any, regrets. I am truly grateful for having her in my life and the experiences we shared together.

Life is too short for any of us to hold hatred or grudges in our hearts. Life was meant to be protected, cherished, and nurtured. What do you think would happen if we could instill these beliefs in our children today? I'll tell you what'll happen: they'll grow spiritually, mentally, and emotionally. Look, our youth are headed on a self-destructive course, especially our young men. And our young women aren't too far behind them. We can no longer afford the brainwashing to continue that's happening to our youths.

It's time to take action. It's time to stop the brainwashing that's taking place in the public school system, the internet, movies, and TV programs. All of these systems, devices, TV programs, and movies are programming their very easily manipulated, impressionable minds to fall for an illusory reality and accept it as truth. The bottom line is this: public schools have been failing to not only educate and nurture our children, they've failed to protect them. I'm living proof of that. I shared some of that information with you in the first part of my book. It's time to hold the public schools and our government responsible for all the continued physical and emotional damage they have been inflicting and continue to inflict on our children. If it's true that every American has the right to life, liberty, and the pursuit of happiness, then why is this atrocity, this abomination to our children continuing to happen? And why or when did our schools become a political instrument to destroy our children? There has to be an end to all of this. We need to protect our children's minds and guide them down the right long narrow road that will instill in them a strong moral and ethical character.

We have way too many young, impressionable, fatherless children seeking guidance from complete strangers who more than likely have a hidden agenda to brainwash all of our children. When we allowed the youth in America to be influenced by TV programs like the Jerry Springer Show, that was the beginning of everything we're witnessing in America and the world today. For a nation without morals, ethics, and godly principles will eventually meet its own inflicted doom. We must all work diligently to get back to doing the right thing. Our star athletes and our movie stars must set the right examples on and off the job. Like it or not, you are the very ones that America's younger generation looks up to. You're either a part of the problem or part of the solution to the problem. Isn't it about time you really showed your fans just how important they really are to you? I think it is, don't you?

Think about how you're going to feel once you start to do this. Maybe you'll even write a book about it? Or even become a public speaker who speaks at public schools, educating these lost kids by planting a seed of true wisdom for the future generations to come, which in turn creates positive role models for them to look up to. Our world is getting faster and faster. We have no time for anyone in this day and age. We all need to start asking ourselves what happened to us, why did it happen, and who's pulling the strings to orchestrate these puppet master crescendo performances that are fooling the masses of young, impressionable minds into submission, working towards transforming our world into total chaos and confusion. The stage was set a long time ago. This is nothing new. It's just becoming acceptable through the brainwashing programming techniques on the internet.

It's time for all of us to unite and become the superheroes. It's time to pull back the curtain just like Toto did in *The Wizard of Oz* and expose these cowardly puppet masters for who they really are. I know what you're thinking: how do we do that, right? It's simple. It's as simple as you picking up your phone and sending a text. United we stand, divided we fall. Unity is the key that will instill us all with the courage to finally pull back the curtain and expose everything.

However, we must always remember to put God first. In doing so, we will find answers to living a life of simplicity, which is what we were all meant to do in the beginning. By teaching only love in its purest form, which can be done even on the internet. Look, social media is being used to attempt to manipulate us all. We type something, someone disagrees, then someone replies, usually with anger and hostility in their response. So how do you combat that? You don't. That's the key. You simply ignore them.

On the internet, this can actually work. In real life, it can be a different story. Trust me, I learned this lesson a long time ago. My parents said, "Ignore them and they'll leave you alone." Maybe for their generation that was the case then. But not for mine. The baby boomer generation was facing challenges that none of us had been prepared to face.

Sure, we learned to adapt to certain things and situations throughout life. But what we didn't learn about and needed so desperately to learn was to teach only love. If we'd learned this, then everything else would have easily just slipped right into place. For love truly does conquer all. It knows no fear, hatred, violence, or regrets. For love is beyond the shadow of a doubt the most powerful force in the universe.

Teach only love and witness a new and more prosperous and nurturing, beautiful world starting to take form right before your very eyes. There would be no more suicides or any unnecessary emotional or physical pain.

There would only be unity, peace, and tranquility in our world.

When the Knights Templars were created, what ignited their interests to serve all Christian pilgrims? The answer: to protect travelers visiting sites in the Holy Land while carrying out their military duties laid out before them by Pope Honorius II, who wanted them to protect and defend the Roman Catholic Church and the Pope. Pope Honorius II inadvertently created the Knights Templar, who originally were monks. Pope Honorius II knew they would willingly do it because they truly believed in the cause they were fighting for!

Which indirectly made them heroes of their time. What does a hero do? They protect and defend the rights and livelihoods of those who can't. So why is this important in today's society? What role does it play in our world today that we should continue on with these iconic traditions, traditions that were instilled in the aging baby boomer populace? The answer: those who don't learn from the lessons and traditions of the past are doomed to repeat history over and over again.

Look, I've played all the roles. I've even been called a hero on more than one occasion. I've even been called a faithful disciple (aka knight). Of which I replied, "I'm just a man who was raised based on morals, ethics, and principles, who loved God and his family unselfishly." However, I apparently forgot about loving myself. Self-love, I have learned, is necessary in order for us to grow into a being of light.

I used to go to psychic bookstores and pay psychics money to find answers to my problems, which in the long run cost me a lot financially. I just wanted answers. My life seemed to play out like a yoyo. I kept coming back, spending money on these psychics, and getting no real answers. Which didn't surprise me one bit, because most of them were charlatans, con artists, frauds who were only telling me what I wanted to hear.

I only met one psychic when I was a young man of 22 years of age. She was a waitress and a horse breeder who we all lovingly called Crazy Rosie. She was always so full of positive energy. As soon as she entered the room, you knew she was there. Crazy Rosie was always giving her female coworkers mini psychic readings. I didn't know it at the time, but Crazy Rosie, Reenie, and Janie had set me up just to see if they could get a peek into my future.

They knew I was Catholic, and I believed that psychics were a forbidden taboo. They apparently didn't care.

Long story short, they made a bet with me; I lost. Then I agreed to let her give me a reading. Most of everything she foresaw in regard to me was coming to light. Coming to light means it actually happened. Four of the future events she saw regarding me and my life actually happened.

I didn't know it yet, but from that moment on, my life was never going to be the same. She was right on the money on all counts. How did she know? She said that I had an interest in law, which I did. At the time, I was actually considering becoming a lawyer. Then, for no known reason, she said I'd make a great lawyer, smiled, and said, "You're gonna hate the paperwork, though." For a brief moment, she was completely quiet and suddenly blurted out, "You'd make a great actor."

I laughed and said, "That's definitely never going to happen. Those people are fakes, phonies. They're not real people."

She gave me a knowing smile, then said this: "Never say never. The universe doesn't believe in never." Then she continued and said, "You're going to be getting married to an older, beautiful woman."

I said, "Really? Does she live here in Arizona?"

She said, "I'm getting a yes on that."

Then, she did one more reading. This time, she wasn't smiling. I said, "What is it, Rosie?" She said that she didn't like it when spirit gave her visions like this one. What she saw was my third oldest brother's death. Three weeks after the complete reading, my brother, according to the obituary, somehow exited or fell out of a vehicle and crushed his temple.

After that happened, I went looking for Crazy Rosie. I couldn't find her. It was as if she never existed. Where did she go? If it wasn't for Crazy Rosie's friends at the once-known Grand Inn, I probably wouldn't have believed she was even a real person. She was real, all right. Yet not even her friends knew where she was or how to contact her.

Okay, so you're probably wondering at this point: why is this story about Crazy Rosie even of significance here? Fair enough, so here it is. What if Crazy Rosie was a messenger sent from the great beyond (or if you prefer, Heaven)? Why do I say Heaven? Same reason most people on the planet believe there's a place called Hades or Hell.

Look, it's true, mankind invented religion. Question is, why would they do it? Answer: in one word, here it is—

control. If Jesus Christ truly died for the sins of the world, then why is it that physical churches charge their church members money through a donation basket they pass around on holidays and Sundays?

Answer: church is a business, just like a so-called psychic who sells their talents by charging a donation for their readings. I'm not saying that all churches and psychics are just hustling spiritual suckers. This isn't a judgment call. It's simply an observation of the things I've witnessed in both sectors.

In doing so, I've discovered that both Heaven and Hell live in us all. I've also discovered that God lives in all of us. He resides somewhere between our conscious and subconscious mind. When we realize this, amazing things start to happen to us. We begin to see the world in a different light. Our purpose, our reason for being, our life mission becomes incredibly clear. We've become a hero by our own right. Now it's all finally starting to make perfect sense, isn't it?